Buon Appetito

Buon Appetito

IN HER FIRST BOOK, MY AMALFI COAST, AMANDA TABBERER DESCRIBED HER EXPERIENCES AS SHE LIVED AND LOVED IN HER ADOPTED HOMELAND, WHERE SHE FORGED HER CAREER AS A FASHION STYLIST, WORKING IN MILAN FOR CONDÉ NAST BEFORE MOVING TO POSITANO. SOON SHE ESTABLISHED HER OWN SIGNATURE RETAIL OUTLET FOR DESIGNER WEAR, EXCLUSIVE SCREENPRINTS AND LUXURY VILLA RENTALS ON THE AMALFI COAST. IN HER SECOND BOOK, AMALFI COAST RECIPES, AMANDA OFFERS A STUNNING COLLECTION OF AUTHENTIC LOCAL RECIPES, GENEROUSLY SHARED BY A WONDERFUL VARIETY OF REGIONAL COOKS AND VIP CHEFS, MANY OF WHOM BECAME CLOSE FRIENDS OVER HER 20 YEARS IN THE AREA. AND YES, SHE IS ALSO MAGGIE TABBERER'S DAUGHTER!

I DEDICATE THIS BOOK TO ADOLFO BELLA (1918 – 2007) WHO TAUGHT ME THE JOYS OF COOKING, APPRECIATING AND LOVING THE FOOD OF THE AMALFI COAST

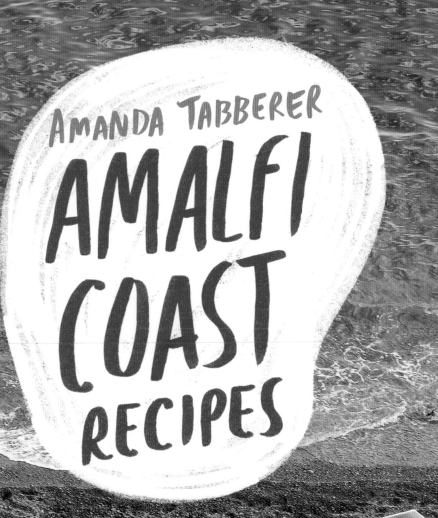

AMANDA TABBERER
AMALFI COAST RECIPES

PHOTOGRAPHY BY
SIMON GRIFFITHS

LANTERN
an imprint of
PENGUIN BOOKS

CONTENTS

PRIMI

SECONDI

INTRODUCTION

My mother started dating my stepfather when I was four years old; it was love at first sight – mine and his, not just Maggie's and his!

Ettore Prossimo was larger than life: tall, elegant and bearded, he would squash his tongue between his teeth when he couldn't control his temptation to bite, squeeze or pinch me. We adored each other. He was known as Rebel or simply Pros to his many friends, but my sister Brooke and I called him Uncle Reb. He married our mother seven years later and became Dad. When I moved to Italy as a young adult he was suddenly Papà until the day he died and broke my heart.

We grew up eating our meals at Uncle Reb's Italian restaurant, Buonasera, nestled in the heart of Sydney's infamous and exciting Kings Cross. At dusk, seated on cans of molasses wedged under the bar's espresso machine, Brooke and I would stuff ourselves with fried oysters and tiny fried potato balls until we looked just like what we were eating! We fell in love with Italian food and our taste has never changed.

The Italian community in Sydney seemed enormous to me and they all knew each other. When my mother Maggie was filming *Beauty and the Beast* on weekends and Buonasera was closed, Uncle Reb would take us out to a busy, steamy and noisy Italian restaurant in Leichhardt that belonged to friends of his and smelt of spicy sausages, rich minestrone and roast pork – it all felt so foreign! We loved the hard marble floor, which looked like a carpet of mortadella. Uncle Reb would order for us and we were never disappointed.

Twenty years later I went to Italy and found my own handsome Italian restaurateur who, oddly enough, would also squash his tongue between his teeth when tempted to bite or squeeze me. (I soon understood that this is a very Italian thing to do.) And so my love affair with a beautiful Italian man and his country's food continued. This time, however, I was seriously submerged in the fairytale town of Positano on the Amalfi Coast and surrounded by hundreds of amazing chefs. It seemed that everyone, from the cleaning lady to the local carpenter, was a Michelin-guide connoisseur when it came to food and the best way to prepare it.

The Amalfi Coast is not only one of the most beautiful areas of the Campania region but also yields some of the finest produce, from its fresh seafood to its mountain-raised game. Knowledgeable cooks are in every kitchen, whether they cook professionally or not, and, apart from enjoying the luxury of excellent fresh produce, they're all passionate about maintaining the traditions passed down to them. They are the protectors of their culinary heritage: it may vary slightly from decade to decade, but it will never lose its solid Neopolitan foundations and will always be passed with pride and joy to the next generation.

In this culinary heritage there is a strong emphasis on fresh seafood of every description, cooked simply and served with fresh local ingredients, such as tomatoes, eggplant, zucchini, capsicum, lemon and artichokes. In the characteristically rustic pasta dishes of the region (many using homemade pasta) the pasta takes centre stage – depending on budget, the simple vegetable or seafood sauces are popular and the pasta is only lightly coated.

Over the twenty years I lived in Italy my connection with food grew daily. My partner was a cook, as were his brother, mother and father. I only realised how much I'd absorbed from them once I returned to Australia and had to fend for myself – I was surprised at the incidental knowledge and skills I'd acquired over my time away. I'd never really had the opportunity to cook while I was there, as the kitchen benches were constantly occupied by busy professional hands. I simply watched, absorbed and prayed they'd let me wash up.

Naturally, 'foodies' hang out with 'foodies'. Most of my partner's friends were great cooks, so an evening with friends at home was often a MasterChef-style cook-off. It was never declared an actual competition, but the competitiveness was fierce and the result was always magnificent.

Good food was expected every day of the year, no matter how simple or humble, and the ingredients had to be the best, whether purchased from a top alimentari (deli), acquired from a friendly local farmer or picked from the side of the road. Time dedicated to preparing meals was a given and there were few shortcuts – the two or three-hour break at lunch isn't just for the siesta.

If you were in the food business and busy preparing meals for others, you'd eat when you could, but it was always the best and tastiest dish from a reliable source, prepared with great skill and love. You'd be comfortably seated with a good glass of wine and never rushed. Unknowingly, the locals of the Amalfi Coast were always great exponents of Slow Food.

Before moving to the jewellery-box Amalfi Coast in the south, I lived and worked for two delicious years in Florence and Milan in the north. There, too, I was constantly surrounded by food. I spent one Thanksgiving in a rundown farmhouse outside Florence with Cristobel Blackman, daughter of the artist Charles Blackman, and a crazy friend Lyle, the son of a preacher man from down south in the US. For an entire day we all sat on a cold rustic kitchen floor with our feet wedged firmly against the old oven door, which was drooping from its hinges, to hold in a sixteen kilogram turkey while it cooked. Passing inebriated friends would occasionally feed us nibbles, pour us some vino or take our place for a bathroom break. I remember that turkey as one of the best I've ever eaten and I'm convinced it was due to the love and time we put into its preparation and cooking.

Another time a good Aussie mate, Simon Miller, son of the well-known entrepreneur Harry Miller, already firmly established in Florence, invited me to meet a wine-distributor friend of his. This friend lived in Piazza della Signoria, right in the heart of Florence, on the top floor of a thirteenth-century building. Not one of the stone stairs resembled another and it was a mountain hike to reach that little attic. Marco de Grazia, today one of Italy's top wine exporters and connoisseurs, awaited our breathless arrival with a big smile, a glass of simple Tuscan red and a juicy heart sandwich (heart is the devon of Tuscany). Yikes, those Florentines sure have a gamey diet! But the day continued into the night with beautiful wines, delicious food and extraordinary music – I believe everyone in Florence plays the guitar and has a wonderful voice . . . or perhaps it just sounds sensational after copious amounts of wine.

By the time I arrived on the Amalfi Coast, my tastes had developed and I was ready for anything. But I found myself dwarfed by the prowess of the local talent and all I could offer was a humble chocolate mousse at my partner's family-run business, Da Adolfo restaurant, where I was a barefoot running waiter. A close girlfriend had given me the recipe many years before, when I was living and working in Paris, the land of the mousse. Surprisingly, the customers adored my mousse served in simple chilled glasses, but the kitchen staff grew to hate me – every glass I used would be invested with a rich flavour of dark chocolate and raw egg and it's almost impossible to remove that eggy taste from a glass. They declared that either the mousse or I had to go. These days I can't even remember the recipe!

Dismantling Da Adolfo beach restaurant at the end of each summer took only a few days, but to rebuild it at the beginning of the season would sometimes take up to three months, depending on the damage the sea had done during the winter months. Either way I had some of the best meals I've eaten in Italy during those long spring months of hard physical work. Between bouts of construction we'd squeeze into the cramped kitchen among the stored deckchairs and anchor lines to whip up a spaghetti con le fave (broad beans are always in season in spring) or a pasta aglio e olio (garlic and oil) or a simple canoe-sized panini (sandwich) stuffed with fried eggplant and dripping with Neapolitan tomato sauce. There were no heart sandwiches in this part of town, which I can't say upset me.

Even today, when I'm hungry but can't for the life of me think what I want to eat, I head to my kitchen and make the simplest spaghetti aglio e olio or pasta al pomodoro (tomatoes). The first bite always settles my soul but sends a little twang of nostalgia through my heart – and I can't quite work out if I'm pining for Positano or its food. Surely it must be both!

For the warm locals of the Amalfi Coast and so many other small Italian communities, the greatest joy lies in sharing wonderful food with as many people as possible. Here are some of the dishes that evoke the most powerful memories for me. I hope you, your family and friends find them as tempting as I do.

PASTA COOKING INSTRUCTIONS
The cooking times given in the recipes are a guide only, and can vary from brand to brand. I generally remove the pasta a good 2–3 minutes before the packet suggests as I like it al dente, and it will continue cooking when added to the hot sauce.

OVEN TEMPERATURES
The recipes were tested using a fan-forced oven. If you are using a conventional oven, set the temperature approximately 20°C higher than is recommended in the recipe.

ANTIPASTI

OCTOPUS AND POTATO SALAD

INSALATA DI POLPO E PATATE

by Rosaria Ferrara

This dish is such a classic in this area that it must be included. Rosaria follows the traditional method of 'dunking' the octopus to curl up the tentacles and tenderise the meat. On the day we shot this photograph, Rosaria's octopus was a little battle worn, with a couple of tentacles missing, but he was screamingly fresh. This is a good sign: he must have been a courageous fighter!

SERVES 6

1 stick celery, roughly chopped
1 carrot, roughly chopped
1 small white onion, roughly chopped
2–3 bay leaves
1 × 600 g octopus, well cleaned (ask your fishmonger to do this)
about 1¼ tablespoons rock salt
400 g potatoes
100 ml extra virgin olive oil
salt
1 tablespoon finely chopped flat-leaf parsley
1 clove garlic, finely chopped
good splash of dry white wine

Put the celery, carrot, onion and bay leaves in a large saucepan, add 2 litres water and bring to the boil. Continue boiling over medium heat for 10 minutes to make a broth.

Take the octopus by the head, with four fingers tucked into it like a handle, and dip it into the boiling broth for 30 seconds. Repeat this another two or three times until the tentacles start to curl, then release the octopus into the broth (this process should stop the octopus becoming hard during cooking). Leave it to boil over medium heat for 30 minutes, adding some rock salt to taste. Test by piercing with a fork – if it pierces easily, it's ready; if it's still hard, let it cook for a little longer. When it's ready, remove it from the water and set aside until it is cool enough to handle with bare hands. Reserve about 250 ml of the broth as you may need it later.

Meanwhile, boil the potatoes in their skins until cooked but not too soft – they should be perky! Leave to cool slightly, then peel and cut into 2 cm dice. Set aside.

Pull each cooled tentacle down lengthways, squeezing at the same time to remove the suction pads and gelatine coating. Chop the flesh into 2 cm pieces.

Combine the octopus and potato in a bowl and dress with the oil, salt, parsley and garlic. Mix well, then finish with a splash of wine to give the salad perfume. If the salad seems a little dry, add some of the reserved broth and toss gently. Serve with amore.

NOTE *To get the most luscious results, you must follow Rosaria's instructions to the letter. It is important that you squeeze each tentacle then pull down firmly, taking away the gelatine and suction pads. This should only be done when the octopus is warm or hot.*

ARTICHOKE AND RICOTTA BALLS

POLPETTE DI CARCIOFI E RICOTTA

by Anna Tizani

Artichokes are my favourite vegetable. Luckily, the Amalfi Coast has an abundant supply when they are in season, and they are considered to be some of the best in Italy. In the area of Paestum, where three majestic Greek temples stand, there are fields and fields of these spiky little devils during April. The locals have a generous repertoire of artichoke recipes (and healing potions – see side note). Anna's ricotta balls are definitely up there with the most scrumptious.

MAKES ABOUT 16 BALLS

3 large artichokes
2 tablespoons extra virgin olive oil
1 onion, roughly chopped
200 g minced veal
salt and pepper
120 ml vegetable stock
200 g fresh ricotta
30 g parmesan, grated
2 egg yolks
1 tablespoon chopped flat-leaf parsley
2 pinches of grated nutmeg
1–2 slices stale white bread, crusts removed
2 eggs
plain flour, for dusting
fresh breadcrumbs made from stale bread (see page 30), for coating
peanut, sunflower or extra virgin olive oil, for deep-frying

To clean the artichokes, break off all the tough outer dark green leaves until you reach the very pale leaves, and trim off any spikes from the top with some scissors. Chop off the stems and shave off the dark green exterior. The insides of these stems are delicious when trimmed well and can also be cut thinly and used in the recipe. Cut the artichokes in half and scoop out the slightly hairy middle (if present), then cut these halves in half again and thinly slice. If the artichoke starts to go brown, don't worry as it will soon be cooked and blended into the polpette mix.

Heat the oil in a large frying pan over medium heat, add the onion, veal, salt and pepper and cook for about 4 minutes or until the veal is lightly browned. Reduce the heat to low, add the artichoke and stock and cook, covered, for 6 minutes or until the artichoke is tender. If there is too much liquid, increase the heat and simmer, uncovered, until it has reduced. Taste and adjust the seasoning if necessary.

Put the ricotta, parmesan, egg yolks, parsley, nutmeg, salt, pepper and 1 slice of bread in a blender. If the mixture is too runny, add another slice of bread.

Transfer the ricotta mixture to a bowl, add the artichoke mixture and combine well. Cover with plastic film and place in the fridge until cool.

Whisk the eggs in a shallow bowl. Place a little flour in another bowl, and the breadcrumbs in a third bowl.

Form the artichoke and ricotta mixture into golf-ball-sized balls. Pass them lightly through the flour, then the beaten egg and finally the breadcrumbs, shaking off any excess.

Half-fill a medium deep frying pan with oil and heat over high heat until very hot but not smoking. Add the artichoke balls and cook, keeping them moving, until they are uniformly golden. Remove with a slotted spoon and drain on paper towels.

Serve just as they are or with fresh mixed salad.

ADOLFO, MY SON'S GRANDFATHER, WOULD EAT BOILED ARTICHOKES AND DRINK THE LIQUID HE COOKED THEM IN FOR DAYS WHEN HE FELT HE HAD OVERINDULGED IN RICH FOOD AND WINE. A GREAT LIVER CLEANSER, HE DECLARED!

Rustic dishes like this one are popular on the Amalfi Coast and have been around for many decades, perhaps centuries, because they are made with basic ingredients that everyone can afford. Every household has their own version of pasta and potato bake, and Rosaria's is absolutely divine!

SERVES 12

30 g butter
fresh breadcrumbs made from stale bread (see page 30),
   for lining and sprinkling
2 tablespoons extra virgin olive oil
1 small white onion, diced
700 g potatoes, peeled and cut into 1 cm dice
2 pinches of salt
400 g spaghetti
400 g smoked provola cheese, cut into 1 cm dice
150 g parmesan, grated

BELL PEPPER SAUCE
4 tablespoons extra virgin olive oil
2 medium yellow bell peppers, seeded and sliced
½ white onion, sliced
8 salted capers, rinsed and drained
salt (optional)

Preheat the oven to 180°C (fan-forced). Grease 12 Texas muffin tins with butter, then add a handful of breadcrumbs and turn to coat the tin. Gently shake out any excess crumbs.

Heat the oil in a large saucepan over medium heat, add the onion and cook until softened and transparent. Add the potato and cook, stirring, for 10 minutes or until golden. Pour in enough water to just cover the potato mixture, add the salt and cook, covered, over low heat for 5–6 minutes or until the potato is tender. Using a wooden spoon, gently squash some of the potato against the side of the pan.

Snap the spaghetti in half and then in half again. Add more water to the potato mixture if needed and bring to the boil. Add the spaghetti and cook, covered, for 6–7 minutes or until al dente, stirring frequently so it doesn't stick to the bottom. Check the water levels again and add a little more hot water if the mix is too dry. Alternatively, if you have too much liquid, remove some with a ladle. The consistency should be creamy but the pasta should be al dente.

Stir in the provola and parmesan, then spoon the mixture into the prepared tins and sprinkle with breadcrumbs. Bake for about 35 minutes or until the tops are golden.

Meanwhile, to make the sauce, heat the oil in a small saucepan over low heat, add the bell pepper, onion and capers and cook, covered, for 10 minutes. Transfer to a blender and puree until smooth. Taste and add salt if needed.

Remove the pasta and potato cakes from the oven and leave for about 10 minutes before turning out onto plates. Serve with the bell pepper sauce.

NOTE *I have had so many combinations of pasta and potato while living in Italy and have never been disappointed. In this delicious concoction, the provola cheese gives a punchy flavour referred to as a 'salt' in bocca (a bounce in the mouth)!*

PASTA AND POTATO CAKES WITH SMOKED PROVOLA WITH BELL PEPPER SAUCE

TORTINA DI PASTA E PATATE CON PROVOLA AFUNICATA CON LA SALSA DI PEPERONI

by Rosaria Ferrara

Aldo CASO

POSITANO, PROFESSIONAL CHEF

Aldo is an excellent chef and has been cooking for one of my favourite trattorias for more than a decade and in Positano for more than thirty-five years. He lives a twenty-minute Vespa ride from Positano and travels to and fro four times a day for his lunch and dinner shifts. He's the quiet man on the bike nobody ever seems to notice, but *everyone* eats his food, from locals all year round to thousands of tourists during summer. His workplace is Grottino Azzurro, the trattoria at the bus stop at the top of Positano – undoubtedly the iconic establishment in town.

His food is good, classic, no-frills Neapolitan cuisine. I've known Aldo for years and his quiet nature led me to believe that my chances of prying a recipe from him for this book would be slim. His generous spirit got the better of him, though, and we spent a few funny days in the restaurant kitchen rolling, tossing, kneading and chopping.

Aldo's first job was in a local Positano hotel kitchen at the tender age of fifteen. Today he continues to keep it simple, preparing some of the most appetising dishes from his tiny kitchen – his oven is a one-dish wonder that looks like a microwave. He told me that his favourite dish is almost boneless, delicately flavoured sea bass. I expected a detailed, tricky recipe but, like so many good cooks,

Aldo likes to keep it simple: just steamed, with a drizzle of good-quality extra virgin olive oil, no salt. He believes that if the fish is fresh and of prime quality, no other flavours are required.

During his well-deserved break midweek, he enjoys cooking for his wife and two teenage boys. He even finds time to indulge his passion for growing his own potatoes, tomatoes, herbs, olives, and grapes for his special artisan wine. It's a far cry from the bustling bus-stop trattoria at the top of Positano.

ALDO'S RECIPES

This is one of the nicest naughty dishes around. It is interpreted a thousand different ways all over Italy but particularly around the region of Campania. What could be more tempting than an open sandwich of deep-fried mozzarella on toast? Aldo has worked out that one slice of bread is better than the traditional two, which has the added bonus of cutting a few calories . . . Wicked but utterly delicious!

SERVES 6
750 ml extra virgin olive oil or sunflower oil
2 eggs
1½ tablespoons grated parmesan
salt and pepper
plain flour, for dusting
6 slices of day-old fior di latte (cow's milk mozzarella)
6 slices of day-old compact bread, crusts removed

Pour the oil into a 20 cm deep non-stick saucepan – not too wide, as the level of oil must be high. Heat over medium heat until the oil is about 200°C. Test by dropping in a little egg mixture – if it sizzles, it's ready.

Meanwhile, whisk together the eggs, parmesan, salt and pepper in a shallow bowl. Place a little flour in another bowl.

Put the mozzarella slices on the bread slices. Lightly dust with flour, then coat in the egg mixture. Working in batches of no more than two at a time, add the bread and cheese bundles to the pan and cook for about 1 minute or until golden. If the top is still pale, turn it over and cook until both sides are golden, then eat piping hot!

NOTE *For best results, use bread and mozzarella that are at least a day old. They will have dried out a little, giving a crisper finish.*

FRIED MOZZARELLA ON TOAST

MOZZARELLA IN CARROZZA

by Aldo Caso

WHEN DEEP- OR PAN-FRYING, GOOD COOKS NEVER OVERCROWD THEIR PANS, AND FOR A GOOD REASON: THE OIL IN AN OVER-FILLED PAN WILL AUTOMATICALLY LOSE HEAT AND PENETRATE THE FOOD MORE READILY, MAKING THE FOOD GREASY. COOKING IN BATCHES IS THE TRICK!

STUFFED OXHEART TOMATOES

POMODORO SORRENTINO IMBOTTITO

by Consiglia Giudone

Italians seem to maintain a healthy appetite regardless of the weather, and it surprised me that this dish was so popular at our restaurant during the hot summer months. People would so often opt for warm soups, stews, pasta bakes or hearty stuffed vegetables, while sitting around the beach in wet swimmers in searing temperatures. I guess the two-hour nap after lunch took care of their digestion!

SERVES 6

6 large oxheart tomatoes
2½ tablespoons extra virgin olive oil, plus extra for cooking
½ white onion, finely chopped
200 g arborio rice
500 ml boiling water
50 g salted capers, rinsed, drained and finely chopped
10 basil leaves, finely chopped
1 anchovy under olive oil or salt, rinsed well and finely chopped
50 g black and green olives, finely chopped
salt
150 g day-old fior di latte (cow's milk mozzarella), cut into 6 cubes

Preheat the oven to 180°C (fan-forced).

Carefully cut the top off each tomato, then set these 'lids' aside. Keeping the tomatoes intact, scoop out their pulp with a spoon and reserve.

Heat the oil in a deep frying pan over medium heat, add the onion and cook until softened. Add the rice and stir until coated in the oil, then add the reserved tomato pulp and the boiling water. Cook for 10 minutes or until the rice is half-cooked. Remove the pan from the heat and leave the rice mixture to cool for 10 minutes. Stir in the capers, basil, anchovy, olives and salt, to taste.

Spoon the rice mixture into the tomato shells and poke a cube of mozzarella into the middle of each one. Cover with the tomato lids.

Pour a little oil into a baking dish, add the stuffed tomatoes in a single layer and drizzle with a little more oil. Bake for 25 minutes or until tender.

IN SUMMER, LIFE ON THE AMALFI COAST REVOLVES AROUND FOOD AND THE BEACH.
BUT THERE IS A FLIP-SIDE: THE LATTERI MOUNTAINS. WATCH THE LOCALS —
ON HOT DAYS, THEY WILL OFTEN HEAD UP INTO COOLER, GREENER AREAS.
ALMOST EVERY SEASIDE VILLAGE ON THIS COASTLINE IS FLANKED BY
A LUSCIOUS GREEN MOUNTAIN WAITING
TO BE DISCOVERED.

STUFFED BELL PEPPERS

PEPERONI IMBOTTITI

by Angela Giannullo

Bell peppers in this area are sweeter than anywhere else in the world, which could be why the locals have so many ways to prepare them. Angela's stuffed peppers are a standout. I offer them here as an antipasto recipe, but seriously, if they are big and juicy enough, then just one is a perfect vegetarian secondo which won't leave room for even the tiniest spoonful of gelato!

SERVES 8

8 medium red, yellow and/or green bell peppers
3 slices day-old ciabatta bread, crusts removed if liked
300 g mozzarella, cut into small dice
50 g green olives, seeded and roughly chopped
50 g black olives, seeded and roughly chopped
2 tablespoons salted capers, rinsed and drained
¼ teaspoon white pepper
2 anchovies under olive oil or salt, rinsed well and finely chopped
5 basil leaves, roughly chopped
1 clove garlic, finely chopped
1 egg, lightly beaten
4 tablespoons extra virgin olive oil
salt
fresh breadcrumbs made from stale bread (see page 30), for sprinkling

Grill the whole peppers over a naked flame (or cook them in a preheated 220°C fan-forced oven for 20–30 minutes) until the skin is blistered and burnt but the flesh is still al dente. Place them in a plastic bag and allow to cool and sweat slightly, then peel away the skin.

Preheat the oven to 190°C fan-forced.

Briefly soak the bread in water, then squeeze out the water and cut the bread into small dice. Place in a bowl with the mozzarella, olives, capers, pepper, anchovies, basil, garlic, egg and oil and combine well.

Cut each bell pepper into four even pieces and place on a flat surface, skin-side down. Sprinkle very lightly with salt (there is no need for salt in the filling because of the capers and anchovies).

Put about a tablespoon of the filling onto each piece of pepper and roll up firmly but gently. You will need kitchen string or toothpicks to close them. Arrange them snugly in a baking dish in a single layer, with the seam-side down. Sprinkle with breadcrumbs and bake for 30 minutes or until warmed through. Eat hot, warm or cold – they are unbelievably good!

BELL PEPPERS WITH CAPERS AND OLIVES

PEPERONI CON CAPERI E OLIVE

by Mario Rispoli

This dish is a classic in this region of Italy. The sweetness of the peppers is balanced beautifully by the salty capers and olives. Perhaps not one of the prettiest dishes once you have added the breadcrumbs, but this is an antipasto or side dish fit for a king! A sensational accompaniment for any meat or fish course.

SERVES 6

120 ml extra virgin olive oil
pinch of fresh or dried chilli
1 clove garlic, peeled and squashed
1 tablespoon salted capers, rinsed and drained
6 mixed olives, pitted and roughly chopped
6 red bell peppers, seeded and cut into strips
5 tablespoons fresh breadcrumbs made from stale bread (see page 30)

Heat the oil in a large deep frying pan over medium heat, add the chilli, garlic, capers and olives and cook, stirring, for a few minutes until the garlic is golden.

Remove the garlic clove, then reduce the heat and add the red pepper. Cook, stirring, for 30 minutes until the red pepper is tender, adding a little water every so often. Just before serving, fold in the breadcrumbs. Serve hot.

FRIED PUMPKIN

ZUCCA FRITTA

by Agatina Semprevivo

Pumpkin is widely eaten up and down the Amalfi Coast. You will find it in soups, risottos, pasta dishes, bakes, side dishes, antipasti – even the great American pumpkin pie! This very simple recipe is perfect to accompany any main course but can also be enjoyed as a delicious antipasto.

SERVES 6

100 ml extra virgin olive oil
1 small fresh or dried chilli, left whole or roughly chopped
   (depending on how much heat you like)
pinch of salt
250 g Queensland Blue or butternut pumpkin (squash),
   peeled and cut into slices less than 1 cm thick
1 dessertspoon good-quality balsamic vinegar
flat-leaf parsley leaves, to garnish

Heat the oil in a large frying pan over medium heat until it is very hot but not smoking. Add the chilli and salt, and then the pumpkin slices and cook until golden brown on both sides.

Remove and drain on paper towels. Arrange the pumpkin on a serving plate, then dress with the vinegar and garnish with parsley. Serve warm.

CUTTLEFISH AND CELERY WITH WALNUTS

SEPPIE E SEDANI CON GHERIGLI DI NOCE

by Giuliano Donatantonio

Cuttlefish is a classic antipasto in these parts, but Giuliano's idea of coupling it with celery, walnuts and lemon juice make this a joy to the palate. The magic is in the combination of textures: the crunch of the celery and walnuts and the melt-in-your-mouth softness of the cuttlefish make it the perfect summer starter to any meal.

SERVES 4

600 g cleaned cuttlefish without the tentacles
4 sticks celery, well washed
1 teaspoon salt
juice of 2 small lemons
3–4 tablespoons extra virgin olive oil
10 walnuts, roughly chopped
3 tablepoons roughly chopped flat-leaf parsley
pepper (optional)

Boil the cuttlefish in salted water for 20 minutes. Drain, then immediately plunge the cuttlefish into iced water to stop the cooking process. When cool, pat dry and cut into long thin strips.

Meanwhile, shave long strips of celery with a potato peeler and place in iced water so they curl and become crunchy.

Place the celery and cuttlefish in separate bowls and dress them both with salt, lemon juice and oil.

Make a bed of dressed celery in four small bowls or one large bowl and arrange the cuttlefish on top. Sprinkle over the chopped walnuts and parsley and finish with a twist of black pepper, if desired. Summer bliss!

Giuliano DONATANTONIO

MINORI, RESTAURANT CHEF

Giuliano is one of three sons of a local fisherman, and all three are chefs. He knows more about what comes out of the sea than anyone I've ever met, and is driven to develop new and exciting dishes using traditional flavours.

A passionate soul, he sometimes works twelve-hour days during the summer season, tossing pasta and pulling fish from his ovens. Like his father, he's a dedicated fisherman, spending entire nights at sea, even in the dead of winter.

Giuliano has ties to Normandy in France, where he'd one day like to open an Italian seafood eatery, but for now he's happy to learn and grow within the ancient walls of his home town Minori, making wonderful food for the four-star Hotel Villa Romana. He also finds time to give cooking lessons to hotel guests.

A wonderful Christmas Eve dish his grandpa taught him has become his favourite meal to prepare for others: spaghetti alla conventuale (spaghetti of the convent). He says, 'All you need to make a success of this dish are nuts, anchovies, cheese and people!' His favourite dish to eat is pasta fagioli e cozze (pasta with beans and mussels), a classic treat from the mountains and the sea.

With ten years' experience at the Hotel Villa Romana, Giuliano sometimes has back-to-back lunch and dinner shifts, but he always finds time to cook for his family – he's a truly dedicated husband and nurturing father. 'When you love what you do, somehow you *make* the extra hours in the day,' he says. Nothing beats a dedicated father who can cook like a god!

GIULIANO'S RECIPES

Cuttlefish and celery with walnuts.. 22
Iconic Amalfi Coast fish soup........ 155
Schiaffoni with cuttlefish
 alla Saracena 108
Spaghetti of the convent.............. 86

Lucia BORRIELLO

VIETRI, OWNER / CHEF OF RISTORANTE 34 'DA LUCIA'

Lucia has always been regarded as a great chef in her home town, but it wasn't until six years ago that she found the courage to open her own little eatery in one of the quaintest piazzas in her ceramic-framed city of Vietri. The result is rustic, simple and delicious. Lucia is the protagonist in this kitchen – a one-man band with a great back-up team of loved ones – and the restaurant has become very popular with both locals and tourists. She is sweet-natured, quietly spoken and a lover of excellent local cooking, but running a restaurant is a big bite to take and I wonder if it may give her occasional heartburn! As long as Lucia is in the kitchen this will always be my choice of eateries in Vietri.

LUCIA'S RECIPES

Cuttlefish and onions in white wine.. 26

These tantalising little sardines are a treat, with their smoky stuffing of provola and prosciutto. Ada actually won first prize for this recipe while participating in a cooking school in Sorrento! Serve them straight away to make the most of the crispy coating and melted cheese.

MAKES ABOUT 10

500 g (about 10) fresh sardines (or fresh anchovies if you can find them)
150 g smoked provola cheese, cut into thin strips
150 g prosciutto, thinly sliced (about 10 slices)
2 eggs
½ teaspoon salt
1 tablespoon roughly chopped flat-leaf parsley
plain flour, for dusting
500 ml peanut oil

Rinse the sardines well under cold running water, then open them like butterflies and remove the main backbones and heads. Pat dry with paper towels.

Place a piece of provola and a slice of prosciutto on one half of each sardine, then fold the remaining half back over the filling.

Whisk together the eggs, salt and parsley in a shallow bowl. Place a little flour in another bowl. Dust the sardines in the flour, shaking off any excess, and then coat in the beaten egg mixture.

Pour the oil into a large deep frying pan and heat over high heat until very hot but not smoking. Add the sardines and cook until golden on both sides. This will happen quite quickly so keep an eye on them. Remove and drain on paper towels, then eat immediately.

PREGNANT FRESH SARDINES

SARDINE INCINTE

by Ada D'Urzo

ALWAYS MAKE SURE YOUR OIL IS FRESH (NEVER REUSED) AND WELL HEATED BEFORE DEEP-FRYING OR EVEN PAN-FRYING. THIS WAY, LESS OIL WILL PENETRATE THE FOOD YOU ARE PREPARING AND THE RESULTS WILL BE CRISPER!

THESE LITTLE 'FISHY' MORSELS ARE THE PERFECT ANTIPASTO TO WHET YOUR APPETITE FOR LUNCH AT ADA'S BEACHSIDE RESTAURANT AFTER A MORNING SWIMMING AND BASKING IN THE SUNSHINE.

PASTA FRITTERS

FRITTELLE DI PASTA

by Agatina Semprevivo

Fritters are a staple dish all over Italy – it's their version of a simple sandwich – but there are some women who have the magic touch when it comes to preparing them. Agatina is one of them. Anything to do with a little oil in a pan and she is the expert!

MAKES 12-14 FRITTERS

250 g good-quality fresh egg tagliatelle
2 tablespoons thick cream
200 ml milk
180 g strong plain flour (such as Italian '00')
80 g parmesan, grated
1 teaspoon salt
1 teaspoon pepper
3 eggs
150 ml peanut oil
radicchio leaves, to serve

Bring about 2 litres of salted water to the boil in a large saucepan. Add the tagliatelle, squeezing them once as you drop them in the water to break them up. Cook until very al dente (about 3 minutes), then drain and rinse immediately under cold running water.

Combine the cream, milk, flour, parmesan, salt, pepper and eggs in a large bowl, then add the pasta and mix well.

Heat the oil in a large frying pan over medium heat until hot but not smoking. Working in batches, add a heaped tablespoon of mixture for each fritter and cook for 3 minutes or until golden. Gently turn the fritters over and cook for another 3 minutes, then remove and drain on paper towels. Repeat with the remaining mixture. Serve with radicchio leaves for colour.

NOTE *This can be prepared as one large fritter or many smaller ones (as here), depending on your fritter-tossing skills. The smaller individual ones are easy to turn, but for the larger one you'll need a lid to help shuffle it out of the pan, flip it and then return it to the pan to cook the other side.*

CUTTLEFISH AND ONIONS IN WHITE WINE

SEPPIE E CIPOLLA

by Lucia Borriello

The delicate flavour of the cuttlefish contrasts beautifully with the sweetness of slow-cooked onion in this dish. It's a perfect example of Lucia's 'comfort food' without losing its summer freshness.

SERVES 8

200 ml extra virgin olive oil
1 kg white onions, finely chopped
250 ml white wine
salt
4–5 dessertspoons balsamic vinegar
3 small cuttlefish, cleaned and chopped into 1–2 cm pieces
plain flour, for dusting
250 ml sunflower or peanut oil

Heat the olive oil in a medium frying pan over low heat, add the onion and cook until transparent. Add the white wine and cook slowly until it has evaporated. Let the onion mixture cool, then give it a few pumps with a stick blender. Add salt and vinegar to taste and stir until the onion becomes golden.

Lightly dust the cuttlefish pieces with flour. Heat the sunflower or peanut oil in a medium frying pan until very hot but not smoking. Add the cuttlefish piece by piece, then reduce the heat and cook, covered, for 5 minutes. Remove with a slotted spoon and stir gently into the onion mixture. Serve warm.

ROCK BREAD SALAD

CAPONATA ALL'INSALATA

by Agatina Semprevivo

You will find 'caponata' salad all over Italy and it is quite different in every region. The caponata in Campania is generally prepared with hard dried bread (known as freselle) that has been quickly soaked to soften, then dressed like a salad with herbs, tomatoes and oil. The Sicilian version is more like a ratatouille and, although Agatina is originally Sicilian, after 40 years in Positano she prepares her caponata in pure Campania style!

SERVES 6

6 slices 2–3-day-old ciabatta bread
   (or use ready-made freselle – see note below)
400 g oxheart, bullock or good-quality truss tomatoes,
   cut into rough wedges
1 white onion, thickly sliced
200 g rocket leaves
3 good pinches of dried oregano
pinch of salt
100 ml extra virgin olive oil, plus extra if needed

If making your own freselle, preheat the oven to 160°C (fan-forced). Put the bread slices on a baking tray or directly on the rack in the oven and bake for 15–20 minutes or until hard and golden. Remove and leave to cool. Put the hard bread or freselle under cold running water for a few seconds (they should soften immediately), then break up the bread into large bite-sized chunks.

Combine the tomato, onion and rocket in a bowl and dress with the oregano, salt and oil. Toss gently to coat.

Add the bread to the salad and toss well, adding extra oil if required (the bread can really soak it up). Eat immediately with a chilled glass of Falanghina or Fiano from Avellino, Campania.

NOTE *If you don't have time to make your own freselle, you can buy them from good Italian grocers. The rock bread with fennel (see page 46) also work really well in this recipe.*

THIS IS OUR FAVOURITE DISH TO TAKE TO SEA ON A HOT SUMMER'S DAY. IT'S REFRESHING AND CAN BE PUT TOGETHER AT SEA WITH LITTLE FUSS. PEOPLE OFTEN ADD THEIR OWN PERSONAL TOUCH, SUCH AS FRESH BOCCONCINI, LOCALLY JARRED TUNA CHUNKS AND LIGHTLY GRILLED EGGPLANT — ALL GREAT ADDITIONS TO THIS CLASSIC RECIPE.

Like his father Adolfo, Daniele is a great lover of artichokes and has been cooking them for decades. In Italy, the Easter period produces the best and most succulent artichokes. I always knew when Adolfo was looking for a good liver cleanse after overindulging in rich food and wine as we would be served artichokes for lunch! Daniele also swears by their blood-cleansing properties. Whatever the reason for eating them, Daniele's recipe is mouth-watering.

SERVES 6

6 young, firm artichokes
6 slices stale bread (ciabatta is good)
2 cloves garlic, finely chopped
small bunch flat-leaf parsley, finely chopped
60 g parmesan, grated
1 anchovy under olive oil or salt, rinsed well and finely chopped (optional)
salt
90 g pancetta, cut into 6 thick chunks (about 3 cm × 3 cm × 1 cm)
3 potatoes, peeled and cut into 3 cm dice
2½ tablespoons extra virgin olive oil

Without cutting with a knife, remove all the internal spikes and hairs from the artichokes (a melon scooper is good for this). Snap off all the woody external leaves and the stem to create a flat base. You can use at least 8 cm of the stem in this recipe, just shave away the woody dark-green exterior and use the internal part. Turn them upside down on a hard surface and give them a good whack with the palm of your hand to open the inside where the stuffing will go. If they are super firm, try soaking them for an hour or two in cold water and they will be easier to open.

Soak the bread in cold water for a few minutes, then squeeze it out, leaving just a little water in the bread.

Combine the bread, garlic, parsley, parmesan and anchovy (if using) in a large bowl. Taste and add salt if needed.

Shake the artichokes free of water, then open the centres well and stuff with the bread mixture, packing it down quite firmly. Make sure the artichokes can sit snugly in a saucepan in a single layer without toppling over, then place a chunk of pancetta on top of each one.

Check and make sure all the stalks have been removed. You can then shave off the dark-green woody skin and drop the inside white pieces around the bottom of the pan. Pack the artichokes neatly into the pan, with only a little space between each. Drop in the potato dice and artichoke stems and pour in enough water to just cover the potato. Drizzle the oil over the artichokes.

Cover and bring to the boil, then reduce the heat to low and cook for 30–45 minutes or until the artichokes are tender when pierced with a fork or skewer. Serve warm with the diced potato.

NOTES *You can leave out the potatoes if you are serving this as an antipasto – the bread stuffing is all you need. But if you are preparing the artichokes as a secondo, the potatoes help round out the meal. I can't tell you how good they taste!*

According to Daniele, artichokes only turn brown when they have been cut with a knife! So in this recipe it's better to snap off the leaves and stem without a knife in sight.

STUFFED ARTICHOKES

CARCIOFI IMBOTTITI

by Daniele Bella

ALWAYS RINSE FRESH ARTICHOKES IN HOT WATER TO HOLD THEIR CHARTREUSE COLOUR AND DO <u>NOT</u> RUB THEM WITH LEMON OR YOU WILL COMPLETELY ALTER THEIR FLAVOUR. THE HOT WATER WILL MAKE THEM CRISP AND STOP THEM GOING BROWN.
IF YOU ADD A TEASPOON OF FLOUR WHILE SOAKING THEY WILL HOLD THEIR CHLOROPHYLL COLOUR!

SARDINE RISSOLES

POLPETTE DI SARDINE FRESCHE

by Rosaria Ferrara

The local sardines have a slightly fishier flavour than the adored fresh anchovies served abundantly on the Amalfi Coast, and these polpette can be made with either. I would not suggest jarred or packaged anchovies as they would be too strong.

SERVES 6

500 g fresh sardines
200 g crustless stale sourdough
1 egg, lightly beaten
100 g parmesan, grated
1 tablespoon roughly chopped flat-leaf parsley,
    plus extra to garnish
1 clove garlic, finely chopped
salt and pepper
2 tablespoons fresh breadcrumbs made from stale bread
    (see note below)
plain flour, for dusting
700 ml peanut oil
lemon slices, to serve

Remove the heads from the sardines, then split them in half and remove the backbone and tail. (If preferred, you can ask your fishmonger to do this messy little chore for you.) Rinse the fillets well to remove the blood and innards, then finely chop with a sharp knife.

Soak the bread in a bowl of cold water for a few minutes and then squeeze it out well. Transfer to a large bowl, then add the chopped sardines, egg, parmesan, parsley, garlic, salt and pepper and mix with your hands to make a paste. If the mix is too soft, add 1–2 tablespoons breadcrumbs. Form the paste into golf-ball-sized balls and squash down slightly. Lightly dust the rissoles in flour, shaking off any excess.

Pour the oil into a medium frying pan and heat over medium heat until very hot but not smoking. To check for the correct temperature, hold a toothpick in the oil for a minute – if the oil starts to make small bubbles around the toothpick, the oil is ready.

Working in batches of no more than six, add the rissoles to the pan and fry for about 3 minutes each side until golden and heated through. If you cook them in larger batches you will overcrowd the pan, which will reduce the heat of the oil, causing the rissoles to absorb more oil and become soggy. Remove and drain on paper towels. Serve hot with lemon slices and, if you like, a crisp green salad.

NOTE *These scrumptious little rissoles of fish can be prepared ahead of time or just before serving. As with most things small and fried, kids will devour them! Unlike a plate of whole sardines . . .*

FRESH BREADCRUMBS *Commercial brands of breadcrumbs have very little flavour and are therefore not commonly used in the south of Italy. It is much better to make your own. Keep your old ciabatta (or any other bread) for a few days or a week until it is nice and hard. Cut it into slices and then toast it. Leave to cool, then put it in a blender and process into breadcrumbs – don't add any seasonings or flavourings. Leave it plain. Presto! You have delicious homemade breadcrumbs that will keep in a sealed jar in the fridge for at least a month. The toasting is the trick: if you do not toast the bread it will become mouldy.*

KINGFISH CARPACCIO

CARPACCIO D'RICCIOLA

by Pasquale Marino

SOME OF THE BEST TUNA IN THE MEDITERRANEAN COMES FROM THIS AREA, DOWN IN THE FISHING VILLAGE OF CETARA (IRONICALLY, THE JAPANESE WERE ALWAYS THE BEST BUYERS OF CETARA TUNA, AND THEY ARE THE KINGS OF CARPACCIO!). YOU WILL ALSO FIND FANTASTIC KINGFISH, FRESH SQUID AND BABY PRAWNS — ALL DELICIOUS WHEN PREPARED CARPACCIO-STYLE.

I don't remember seeing a lot of fish carpaccio when I first arrived in this area 25 years ago, but today it is as popular as a good bowl of seafood pasta. It makes perfect sense as the local seafood is always screamingly fresh and this is a lovely way to enjoy it during the summer months.

SERVES 6

400 g fresh kingfish or swordfish fillets, cut into 1 cm thick slices
4 tablespoons extra virgin olive oil
juice of 2 lemons
salt and pepper
rocket leaves, to serve

Place the fish fillets between two sheets of plastic film. With a kitchen hammer or temper (a utensil with a flat surface), gently beat the fillets, moving the hammer in an outward motion. Don't make them too thin – they should be about 5 mm thick.

Combine the oil, lemon juice, salt and pepper to make a dressing. Taste and adjust the amount of oil or juice if needed.

Just before serving, dip the fish into the dressing and spread out on a large serving dish. Decorate with rocket leaves, then drizzle with a little more dressing. Serve immediately, otherwise the fish will start to 'cook' in the lemony dressing.

ANCIENT SKEWERS OF MOZZARELLA AND BREAD

SPIEDINO ANTICO PROVATURA

by Carla Rispoli

Everything about this simple dish shrieks ancient history: the stale bread, the mozzarella (or provatura, a slightly stringy buffalo mozzarella typical of the Roman region) and the salty anchovies melted into the butter sauce. Every so often Carla removes her 'pastry chef' hat and opts for the delightful flavours of traditional recipes built on pure simplicity.

SERVES 6

1 loaf stale bread (such as a small ciabatta)
24 slices day-old small mozzarella
100 g butter
12 anchovies under olive oil or salt, rinsed well

Preheat the oven to 200°C (fan-forced).

Cut the bread into 30 slices – they should be 1 cm thick and about the same size as the mozzarella slices. Remove the crusts.

Starting with a piece of bread, thread five slices of bread and and four slices of mozzarella alternately onto each skewer. There will be six skewers in total.

Melt the butter in a small saucepan over medium–low heat, add the anchovies and stir until they have melted into the butter.

Put the bread skewers on a baking tray and bake for about 5 minutes or until the bread is golden and the mozzarella has melted. Keep an eye on them as you don't want the bread to burn or the cheese to melt too much. It should still hold its shape.

Place each skewer on a small plate and dress with the anchovy sauce.

NOTE *You will need six 20 cm wooden skewers for this dish. Soak them in water first so they don't burn.*

Practically every food in Italy has a 'polpetta' version – from meats and fish to pasta, rice and vegetables. But it is completely unacceptable for polpette to be soggy. To avoid this, make sure your frying oil is very, very hot, without smoking or burning. This way, the flavour is locked in but the oil does not penetrate.

EGGPLANT BALLS

POLPETTE DI MELANZANE

by Felice Fiore

MAKES ABOUT 16

170 ml extra virgin olive oil
1 clove garlic, peeled and squashed
large pinch of salt, plus extra for sprinkling
1 kg eggplant (aubergine), peeled and cut into 2 cm dice
pinch of dried oregano
5 basil leaves, shredded
50 g parmesan, grated
100 g mozzarella, finely diced (smoked mozzarella is also good)
4 eggs, lightly beaten
150 g fresh breadcrumbs made from stale bread (see page 30)
about 250 ml peanut oil

Pour the oil into a large frying pan and heat gently over low heat. Add the garlic, salt and eggplant (depending on the size of your pan, you may need to do this in batches). Cover and cook until soft and golden, stirring regularly. Remove from the heat and take out the garlic clove, then return all the eggplant to the pan (if necessary). Add the oregano, basil, parmesan and mozzarella and mix well, then stir in the egg and breadcrumbs. Set aside to cool.

Form the mixture into golf-ball-sized balls.

Heat the peanut oil until very hot but not smoking. The exact amount of oil depends on the size of your pan – it should come at least halfway up the side of the eggplant balls. Add the balls (in batches if necessary) and cook for 7 minutes or until golden and cooked through, turning often. Remove and drain on paper towels. Sprinkle with salt and serve immediately (although they are also delicious served cold).

FOR BEST RESULTS WHEN DEEP-FRYING, USE A COOKING OIL THAT REACHES HIGH TEMPERATURES WITHOUT BURNING AND HAS A NEUTRAL TASTE THAT WON'T INTERFERE WITH THE FLAVOURS OF THE INGREDIENTS. NATURALLY, FRESH OIL IS BEST — DON'T REUSE IT. PEANUT AND SUNFLOWER OILS ARE FAVOURED ON THE AMALFI COAST; GOOD-QUALITY EXTRA VIRGIN OLIVE OIL MAY ALSO BE USED, BUT YOU MAY HAVE TO MORTGAGE YOUR HOUSE — IT'S VERY COSTLY!

Felice FIORE

PRAIANO, DELI OWNER

Trim and energetic, Felice (which means 'happy' in Italian) is a dynamic 70-year-old. She spends her days preparing food for her very busy and demanding family, who come and go at all hours depending on their shift at the well-established family deli. She has energy to burn, doesn't muck around and rarely drinks a drop of wine.

A self-taught cook, Felice has learnt by trial and error during her fifty years in the kitchen. A busy dressmaker for decades, she considered herself lucky to be married to the owner of the best deli in town. At the end of each day she'd raid the deli for any goods that could soon spoil, then rush them home to cook up a storm, inventing and experimenting with new dishes that eventually formed the basis of her creative cuisine. She's never wasted an apple – this is the secret to her success.

Her father and son, who both love the sea, are excellent cooks and adore fresh fish, but Felice isn't mad about fish and so leaves most of the fish cooking to them. Her favourite dish is pasta with zucchini done the simplest way – her way: no garlic, egg or cream; more zucchini than pasta; onions, parmesan and fresh basil.

Her dream day is preparing lunch for about fifty hungry family members and watching them eat. Let's hope they at least help with the washing up!

FELICE'S RECIPES

Pasquale MARINO

PRAIANO, WINE SHOP OWNER

Pasquale is Felice's son, and although he first learnt his kitchen skills in Mama's kitchen, he's definitely refined his cooking in his years of working in one of the top restaurants on the coast. Today he has his own vino outlet under his parents' very successful grocery store in Praiano, and its name says it all: Tutto per Tutti (everything for everyone).

Pasquale has been a qualified sommelier since 1998, but his prowess in the kitchen developed through necessity when he started travelling at the age of eighteen and needed to feed himself. Being used to great food at Mama's table, he'd just keep trying until he got it right. As his involvement with fine foods grew, he enrolled in a rigorous course at the Etoile cooking school of Venice, where he excelled.

His grandfather, like many Praianese, was a devoted man of the sea, spending a good portion of his life fishing alongside his brothers. Pasquale was the pesky kid who'd tag along and, like many local kids, learnt almost by feel to fish and to cook his catch.

His favourite food to prepare is fish under salt, which he taught me many years ago. I've cooked this dish for friends and family many times and enjoyed huge success.

Pasquale dreams of making enough money from a recent vineyard project to be able to donate a good portion to the needy children of Africa. Eventually he'd like to create a small restaurant with excellent wines and a refined degustation menu. I know the Amalfi Coast will embrace it with all its hungry heart.

PASQUALE'S RECIPES

VERA AND BROTHER RHINO

Vera MILANO

PRAIANO, RESTAURANT OWNER

I'd been eating at Vera's family restaurant by the sea, Il Pirata, for many years but never really understood how this little place came to be. In the time I've lived in this area, it's been a disco, a bar, a live-music hangout, and then a restaurant and beach establishment. Today, after decades of work in the fashion industry, Vera has created this little family-run seaside paradise for lunch and dinner.

Vera is a huge part of the business's success: she's confident, takes no bullshit from the odd difficult customer and is generally the boss of the wash. I thought the good-looking guy who worked the floor with her was her husband (turns out he's her brother) and the elderly gentleman watching everything and everyone was just a local seaman (turns out he's her father and at nearly eighty still a lifeguard). And the woman I believed to be a kitchen hand is Vera's mother and co-owner. This is a real family business and everything that comes out of Vera's kitchen has been prepared with great attention to detail and dedication to the cuisine of the area.

Vera grew up in a typical southern Italian household and has always cooked for her family; she absorbed all she could from her mentors. When the family got together for a meal, she'd shop, chop, slice, dice, mix, cook, serve and clean everything with the other women while the men sat around talking about politics and soccer, eating and drinking. 'Thank heavens times have changed!' she says now. Like so many others, Vera is happy that the division of labour is so much more balanced these days: the men often cook, contribute around the house and have even been known to help out with the dishes.

Although Vera doesn't cook in the restaurant, her family's recipes are imprinted in her mind and her chefs are proud to produce them each day. Her favourite dish is scialatielli alla stromboli (homemade pasta with mussels, basil, zucchini, pecorino and pepper). She tells me that this dish was born many years ago as a result of a search for new and exciting regional flavours and that it's still incredibly popular today. This dish is definitely worth a trip to her little Pirata paradise, right on the water in Praiano.

VERA'S RECIPES

CLASSIC POTATO PILLOWS

CROCCHÈ DI PATATE

by Vera Milano

Crocchè di patate are without a doubt one of the most delicious antipasti in Italian cuisine. They are generally the first things to disappear off the buffet table – and if there are kids (or men) around, you'd better get in there quickly. Some are made with mozzarella, others with parmesan or ham, but Vera makes hers with EVERYTHING!

MAKES ABOUT 16

500 g pontiac potatoes
2 eggs, separated
50 g parmesan, grated
50 g pecorino, grated
1 small bunch flat-leaf parsley, finely chopped
100 g ham, finely diced
salt and pepper
200 g mozzarella, cut into small dice
250 g fine fresh breadcrumbs made from stale bread (see page 30)
about 500 ml peanut oil

Boil the potatoes in their skins until tender. Leave to cool slightly, then peel and press through a ricer while still hot. Spread the potato out on a flat surface to cool. When cool, transfer it to a large bowl, add the egg yolks, parmesan, pecorino, parsley, ham, salt and pepper and mix to combine.

Take a tablespoon of the mixture and form it into a long fat finger shape. Push a cube of mozzarella into the middle, then close the mixture over to cover. Repeat with the remaining potato mixture to make about 16 pillows.

Lightly whisk the egg whites in a shallow bowl. Pour the breadcrumbs into another bowl.

Coat the pillows in the egg white and then in the breadcrumbs, shaking off any excess.

Heat the oil in a deep frying pan until very hot but not smoking. Add the pillows in batches (so you don't overcrowd the pan) and cook for about 5 minutes or until golden brown. Remove and drain on paper towels, then serve hot. Don't forget to blow and bite gently, otherwise you may need a fire extinguisher for your tongue! And if you burn your mouth, the rest of your meal will be a mystery.

RISTORANTE IL PIRATA

Gennaro makes everything with such style and class, and this little antipasto is no exception. He always selects the best combination of local produce, and then addresses textures to further refine the dish. Ah! Gennaro is nothing short of an artist when it comes to his antipasti!

SERVES 6

1 kg zucchini (courgettes)
plain flour, for dusting
sunflower oil, for frying
500 g fresh sardine fillets, cleaned (or 1 kg whole sardines, filleted and cleaned)
2½ tablespoons extra virgin olive oil, plus extra for drizzling
1 clove garlic, peeled and squashed
1 × 400 g can good Italian tomatoes
50 g parmesan, grated
100 g mozzarella, cut into 5 mm dice
6 basil leaves

Preheat the oven to 160°C (fan-forced). Line a baking dish with baking paper.

Wash the zucchini and thinly slice lengthways using a mandolin or sharp knife (the slices should be 3–4 mm thick). Dust lightly with flour, shaking off any excess.

Pour plenty of sunflower oil into a large saucepan or wok (Gennaro's preference as he swears by a wok's ability to keep a good heat) and heat over medium-high heat until very hot but not smoking. Add the zucchini strips in batches and cook until just blonde on both sides – not too golden. Remove and drain on paper towels.

Lightly dust the sardine fillets with flour and cook in the hot sunflower oil for 1–1½ minutes or until golden on both sides.

Heat the olive oil in a small saucepan over medium heat, add the garlic clove and cook until golden. Remove the garlic, then add the tomatoes and cook, stirring, over high heat for about 10 minutes.

Place the zucchini strips top to tail on a work surface (like a long train of carriages), until about 30 cm long, overlapping slightly. Place five or six sardine fillets on top (also top to tail). Sprinkle over a little parmesan, then roll up firmly like a sleeping bag. Sit the rolls upright in the baking dish and top each one with a cube of mozzarella. Bake for 10 minutes or until the mozzarella has melted.

Spoon some warm tomato sauce onto each serving plate and put the parmigiana rolls on top. Sprinkle on a little more parmesan, add a drizzle of olive oil and finish with a basil leaf. Ecco! You have a beautifully presented, sophisticated dish with the flavour to match!

ZUCCHINI AND SARDINE PARMIGIANA

PARMIGIANA DI ZUCCHINI E SARDINE

by Gennaro Marciante

GIANT RICE BALLS

ARANCINI DI RISO

by Carla Rispoli

Carla's arancini are famous all over the coast – for both their flavour and size. Regular arancini are generally smaller and can be a bit dry and uninteresting, but Carla's are jam-packed with flavour and actually dissolve in your mouth. Her secret? The base is a full-blown risotto alla Milanese, saffron and all. Try them – you'll be hooked.

MAKES 12
6 eggs
salt and pepper
250 g mozzarella, cut into 12 cubes
150 g fresh breadcrumbs made from stale bread (see page 30)
1 litre peanut oil (more if needed)

RISOTTO ALLA MILANESE
2 litres good-quality beef stock
2½ tablespoons extra virgin olive oil
1 small brown onion, finely chopped
500 g carnaroli rice
1 teaspoon saffron threads
100 g parmesan, grated
30 g butter

To make the risotto, bring the stock to the boil in a large saucepan. Reduce the heat and keep at a low simmer. Heat the oil in a large heavy-based saucepan over medium heat, add the onion and cook until lightly golden. Add the rice and stir until well coated in the oil mixture. Add the hot stock, one ladle at a time, stirring until the liquid has been absorbed before adding the next one. Continue in this way for about 15 minutes or until the rice is cooked but al dente. Dissolve the saffron in 1 tablespoon of hot water and stir in when the rice is cooked and the risotto is thick and creamy. Add the parmesan and butter and stir until melted and well combined, then pour the risotto onto a tray and leave to cool completely.

Lightly beat two eggs and stir into the cooled risotto. Taste and add some salt and pepper if needed. If the mixture is too solid, add a little more water or beaten egg to loosen it up. With wet hands, form into 12 large balls (about the size of a tennis ball). Insert one piece of mozzarella into the middle of each ball and close over with the risotto mix.

Beat the remaining four eggs in a shallow bowl, and put the breadcrumbs in another bowl.

Dip each ball into the beaten egg, then coat well with the breadcrumbs, shaking off any excess. You may have some egg and breadcrumbs left over but you need a decent amount of both to do the job well. Don't be stingy.

Pour the oil into a small but deep frying pan (you'll need enough to just cover the balls). Heat the oil to 160°C or until a cube of bread dropped in the oil browns in 25 seconds. Don't allow the oil to get any hotter or the arancini may burn, and this temperature is perfect to melt the mozzarella in the centre and just heat the rice balls through. Add a few balls at a time (to avoid overcrowding the pan) and cook for 8–10 minutes or until golden. Remove and drain on paper towels. Let them rest for at least 2 minutes before serving.

Light and delicate, zucchini flowers make one of the most enchanting antipasti during their season. On the Amalfi Coast, edible flowers range in size from small and delicate to the jumbo pumpkin flowers. And once they have been stuffed and properly cooked, they are a culinary delight. This is one hell of a classy dish – just like Tanina!

ZUCCHINI FLOWERS AU GRATIN WITH BASIL SAUCE

FIORI DI ZUCCHINE GRATINATI CON LA SALSA AL BASILICO

by Tanina Vanacore

SERVES 6

1 kg fresh ricotta
300 g mozzarella, cut into 5 mm dice
100 g parmesan, grated
8 basil leaves, shredded
2½ tablespoons extra virgin olive oil
salt and pepper
30 medium zucchini (courgette) flowers

BASIL SAUCE

200 g basil leaves
80 g pine nuts
120 ml extra virgin olive oil, plus extra to cover
pinch of rock salt
40 g parmesan, grated
40 g pecorino, grated

TOMATO SALAD

2 oxheart tomatoes, finely diced
3 tablespoons extra virgin olive oil
¼ teaspoon salt
8 basil leaves, finely chopped

To make the basil sauce, wash the basil leaves well and pat dry (make sure you dry them well otherwise your sauce will go black). Place the leaves in a blender or food processor, along with the pine nuts, oil and rock salt, and pulse in very short bursts until just blended. This can also be done in a mortar and pestle if you have the technique and willpower! Stir in the two cheeses, then spoon the sauce into a container and cover with a layer of extra oil to avoid oxidisation. The sauce will keep in the fridge for up to a week.

Preheat the oven to 100°C (fan-forced).

Pass the ricotta through a fine colander into a bowl to remove any lumps. Add the mozzarella, parmesan, basil, oil, salt and pepper and mix well, then transfer to a piping bag

Clean the zucchini flowers by cutting off all the little green leaves at the base and remove the pestle in the middle. Carefully wash the flowers and pat them dry.

Half-fill each flower with the ricotta mix, then twist the end so the stuffing doesn't leak out while they are cooking.

Place the zucchini flowers in a baking dish large enough to fit them in a single layer and bake for 4–5 minutes until gently warmed through.

Meanwhile, to make the tomato salad, combine all the ingredients in a small bowl.

Serve the zucchini flowers straight from the oven with the basil sauce and tomato salad.

THE ZUCCHINI FLOWER SEASON STARTS AT THE BEGINNING OF MAY IN THE NORTHERN HEMISPHERE AND THE BEGINNING OF OCTOBER IN THE SOUTHERN HEMISPHERE.

CONTORNI

ROCK BREAD WITH FENNEL

FRESELLA CON FINOCCHIO

by Valerio Buonocore

This is Valerio's homemade version of my favourite bread in Italy, with the inspired addition of wild fennel seeds. It is as hard as a rock and wonderfully digestible compared with most commercial breads. Dress it with a tomato salad and serve as an antipasto, or soak it and toss it through a generously dressed salad (see page 28). Or simply enjoy it as a crunchy snack or side to accompany your main.

SERVES 6

650 g strong plain flour (such as Italian '00')
350 g rye or wholemeal flour
25 g dried yeast
25 g butter
375 ml cold water
1¼ tablespoons salt
2 tablespoons wild fennel seeds

Place all the ingredients in a large bowl and mix until they all come together. Turn out the dough onto a floured surface and knead for about 7–10 minutes or until smooth and elastic.

Cover with plastic film and leave to rise for 30 minutes.

Form the dough into balls about the size of golf balls, then gently flatten each one into a patty – use your finger and push in an outward movement to keep the round shape until each patty is 5 mm thick.

Now roll up each patty to make rolls about 10 cm long and 5 cm thick. Place the rolls on an oiled baking tray, then cover with a tea towel and leave to rise for 45 minutes.

Preheat the oven to 190°C (fan-forced).

Bake the rolls for 23–24 minutes. Remove and let them cool, then cut them in half lengthways. Reduce the temperature to 100°C, then return the rolls to the oven for 1 hour. This second bake will give them their hardness and durability. Cool and store in an airtight container.

NOTE *Many decades ago rock bread was eaten by the less privileged during hard times, but these days it is found in the pantries of most households or indeed in rucksacks on long voyages, as it has a very long shelf life.*

VALERIO'S ROLLS ARE NOT AS HARD AS SOME I HAVE TRIED – YOU CAN EASILY GET YOUR TEETH THROUGH THEM.
SO THEY WOULD MAKE A WONDERFUL AND FLAVOURSOME CRUNCHY SNACK JUST PLAIN.
OR DRESS THEM AS A BRUSCHETTA.

CONTORNI

GRANDPA'S SALAD

INSALATA DEL NONNO

by Rosetta D'Urso

In my early days in Positano I was a regular at Rosetta's lunch table with her very large and boisterous family. In among all the noise, the person who stood out for me was her Papa, who would sit quietly to one side slowly chopping tiny cubes of fresh ingredients. At first I thought he was making some sort of Neapolitan tabbouleh, but after sampling this enchanting mix, I realised that Rosetta's Papa knew a lot more about food flavours than it first appeared.

SERVES 6

4 large tomatoes (not too mature), cut into 1.5 cm dice
2 large sticks celery, very finely chopped
1 clove garlic, finely chopped
5 basil leaves, finely shredded
½ teaspoon dried oregano
½ small red chilli, finely chopped
¼ green bell pepper, seeded and finely chopped (optional)
100 ml extra virgin olive oil
salt

Place the tomato, celery, garlic, basil, oregano, chilli and green pepper (if using) in a bowl and toss gently together.

Dress with oil and salt just before serving. This is particularly good with any summer fish dish.

NOTE *Don't chop the salad ingredients in advance or all the ingredients will bleed their liquid, leaving you with a gazpacho soup!*

WHENEVER POSSIBLE, I LIKE TO MIX
INGREDIENTS TOGETHER WITH CLEAN HANDS.
THEY ARE INFINITELY MORE EFFICIENT
THAN A WOODEN SPOON OR A FORK,
ESPECIALLY WHEN TOSSING A DRESSED SALAD.
SPEAKING OF SALADS, ALWAYS RIP LEAVES
AND HERBS WITH YOUR FINGERS AS
A KNIFE BLADE CAN CAUSE THEM
TO OXIDISE.

FENNEL AND ORANGE WEDGE SALAD

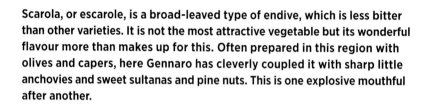

FINOCCHIO E ARANCIO ALL'INSALATA

by Rosaria Ferrara

Oranges from Praiano are well known for their juiciness and flavour (there are three of them embedded on the town's flag!) and this simple salad is one of the best ways to enjoy them. The clean flavours make a wonderful accompaniment to everything from fish to goat. Make it in autumn when oranges and fennel are just coming into their own.

SERVES 6

2 medium fennel bulbs
3 medium oranges, peeled and pith removed
extra virgin olive oil, for drizzling
salt and pepper
80 g pine nuts (optional, but recommended)

Thinly slice the fennel and oranges (on a mandolin if you have one). Cut each orange slice in half and arrange on a platter, topped with the fennel. Dress with oil, salt and pepper and scatter over the pine nuts (if using). Eat with joy!

WILTED ENDIVE

STUFATA DI SCAROLA

by Gennaro Marciante

Scarola, or escarole, is a broad-leaved type of endive, which is less bitter than other varieties. It is not the most attractive vegetable but its wonderful flavour more than makes up for this. Often prepared in this region with olives and capers, here Gennaro has cleverly coupled it with sharp little anchovies and sweet sultanas and pine nuts. This is one explosive mouthful after another.

SERVES 6

600 g scarola, large leaves cut in half
3 tablespoons extra virgin olive oil
2 cloves garlic, peeled and left whole
130 g anchovies under olive oil or salt, rinsed well and drained
100 g pine nuts
100 g sultanas
1 red and 1 green chilli, sliced

Bring 3 litres water to the boil in a large saucepan. Add the scarola and blanch for 3 minutes only.

Meanwhile, heat the oil in a large frying pan over medium heat, add the garlic cloves and cook, stirring, until golden. Remove the garlic. Drain the scarola, reserving 2 tablespoons of the cooking water. Add to the frying pan with the reserved water, anchovies, pine nuts and sultanas and cook for 5 minutes. Transfer to a serving plate and decorate with the chilli.

GENNARO 1 (FRONT OF SCOOTER), GENNARO 2 (BACK OF SCOOTER) AND ACQUA PAZZA STAFF

Gennaro MARCIANTE

CETARA, RESTAURANT OWNER AND CHEF

Like all great chefs, Gennaro has a food motto: 'The story of this coastline teaches us that the ancient fishermen were also farmers; they fished at night and worked the land during the day.' This is what Gennaro's kitchen at Acqua Pazza restaurant is all about.

The son of a local fisherman, Gennaro has followed his motto all his cooking life, from his formal training at the hotelier school in Salerno right up to opening his own little eatery in his tiny home village of Cetara in 1995 with a good mate, also called Gennaro. So we have Gennaro 1 the chef and Gennaro 2 the wine expert and frontman. They're a dynamic duo!

Cetara has always fascinated me: it's the only one of thirteen Amalfi Coast towns that doesn't rely on tourism, yet for its size it has a large number of restaurants. Cetara still lives off its fishing industry, which is mainly concentrated on tuna and fresh anchovies, so Acqua Pazza has a bottle of colatura di alici (fresh anchovy syrup) on each table rather than salt. I adore this quirky twist and Gennaro knows exactly how much to use and where it goes best. Naturally, his favourite dish is spaghetti con la colatura (spaghetti with anchovy sauce).

Gennaro 2 is just as devoted, supporting and supplying some of the best local wines, particularly the boutique wines he's discovered over the years. His favourite dish is their freshly salted anchovies, which are nothing like the salty ones out of a jar. Every dish that comes out of the Gennaros' restaurant is exquisite and delectable!

Today, Gennaro 1 is recognised all over Italy for his innovation in the kitchen, but he has no pretensions: he's basically a lover of all things from the sea. His cuisine is 100 per cent espresso (last-minute prep), which is why he employs some of the best and most capable sous chefs in the area. Gennaro swears by his team.

He has an ongoing love affair with local aromas, herbs and spices, all of which have heavily influenced his cooking. He demands the best ingredients, and has sourced the champion local oils, salts, spices and potatoes. His biggest luxury? He has two brothers who fish only for him – personal fishermen! It's catch of the day every day in Gennaro's kitchen.

GENNARO'S RECIPES

Rosaria FERRARA

POSITANO, PROFESSIONAL COOK

Although Rosaria has long been known around Positano as a great cook, she's only been working as a professional for two years. Her three children are very fussy about their food, scrutinising the finest details and leaving her little room for error. This is perhaps why she's such an excellent cook today.

When Rosaria married twenty-eight years ago, she couldn't boil water for pasta. Her first gnocchi were such a sloppy disaster that she threw them away. Her mother pointed out that she could simply have added a little more flour. And so Rosaria started to learn.

She worked for many years as a shop assistant in her home town of Positano but in recent years, due to her open and friendly nature, has become involved with voluntary work as a representative for Positano in its twin town of Thurnau in Germany. Initially she was invited to demonstrate Amalfi Coast cooking skills. This was a huge success, and her reputation grew in her home town as well. Suddenly she was offered work as a professional cook.

Today she is a jack of all trades, sometimes working as a shop assistant, sometimes cooking professionally and, whenever time allows, flying to Germany to give her cooking classes and keep up diplomatic ties between these two delightful towns. Her passion is definitely Thurnau, and she'd love to open a small Positano-style restaurant there one day, coming to Positano only for holidays, like the rest of us. She's already picked out her little dream venue in Thurnau. Looks like we may have to make the odd trip to Germany as well!

ROSARIA'S RECIPES

Valerio BUONOCORE

RAVELLO, BAKER

I'd been hearing about Valerio's baking prowess for some years, mainly due to his national award-winning breads. Ravello born and bred, Valerio is a largely self-taught talent in the baking world. He told me a while back that the one thing that pushed him to success in this tough and demanding arena was his first employer telling him that he was useless and would never succeed in the baking industry. The employer would soon eat his bread *and* words! Valerio went on to work at Ravello's prestigious five-star Palazzo Sasso hotel for six years, where he refined his world-class baking skills. He also manages to supply freshly baked bread and breakfast cakes to his family's tiny local B&B.

Valerio plans to buy his own massive bread ovens one day and teach children how to get started in the magical art of baking. According to Valerio, 'The drawback is those early-morning starts!' – only the totally dedicated would put up with that. Perhaps this is why the art of baking is slowly disappearing all up and down the Amalfi Coast, along with all the wonderful bakeries.

Valerio was always a squeaky-clean child who hated mess and dirt, and the thought of grubby, sticky fingers never appealed to him. He quickly worked out that the old-fashioned spatula (pallet) with a short handle was the way to go. Today, without a fleck of flour on him, Valerio kneads, folds and churns his dough with a flick of the wrist, just like a professional ping pong player.

When I first arrived all those years ago, there were still a few local bakers in Positano. When we'd rock up in the wee hours of the morning to pick up steaming hot loaves for the day's service at Da Adolfo restaurant, I often noticed the smell of alcohol in the bakehouse. My then partner Sergio told me the bakers were slugging nips on the side as they worked – this demanding enterprise had led them to drink. Thank heavens Valerio is a teetotaller!

VALERIO'S RECIPES

These scrumptious little bread 'bites' are a cloud of bliss on the palate – they are flavoursome, as light as air and, like peanuts, you just can't stop at one. Valerio recently made a batch for me, which he served mid-morning with homemade chocolate liqueur. At that hour, I managed just a sip of liqueur but showed no such restraint with the bread – I ate the lot!

SERVES 8–10

30 g dried yeast
1.25 kg strong plain flour (such as Italian '00'),
    plus extra for dusting
1¼ tablespoons salt
1½ tablespoons sugar
75 g butter, melted
5 cloves garlic, finely chopped
1 tablespoon finely chopped fresh or dried chilli, or to taste
1½ tablespoons chopped flat-leaf parsley, or to taste
1 litre peanut or sunflower oil
rock salt, for sprinkling

Dissolve the yeast in 2½ tablespoons water and set aside for a few minutes until frothy. If it does not start to froth, the yeast is dead and you will have to start again with a fresh batch.

Place the flour, salt, sugar, butter, garlic, chilli, parsley and 650 ml water in a large bowl, add the yeast mixture and mix until it comes together. Turn out onto a floured surface and knead until smooth and elastic. Return the dough to the bowl, cover with plastic film and rest in the fridge for 45 minutes.

On a well-floured board or surface, roll out the dough to a thickness of 5 mm (it's easier if you also flour the top of the dough and the rolling pin). Using a 'bicicletta' (dough divider), pizza cutter or sharp knife, cut the dough into 3 cm squares. Cover with a clean tea towel, then leave to rise for about 30 minutes.

Pour the oil into a large heavy-based pan and heat to 170°C (a cube of bread dropped in the oil should brown in 20 seconds). Add a few bread squares at a time and cook until they are golden, puffed up and floating on the surface. You need patience for this – if you put in too many at once the oil will lose its heat and the bread will not puff up. Sprinkle with rock salt and eat immediately. I dare you to stop at one!

FRIED BREAD

PANE FRITTO

by Valerio Buonocore

FRESH GRILLED VEGETABLES

VERDURA ALLA GRIGLIA

by Consiglia Giudone

These fabulous grilled vegetables are thinly sliced so they take no time to cook and retain all their nutrients. Consiglia has cooked them for overseas visitors for years and they are always 'a bocca aperta' (gobsmacked), which astonishes her! The dish is as easy as falling off a log to prepare if you follow her instructions.

SERVES 6

salt, for grilling
4 medium eggplants (aubergines), cut on the diagonal into 2 cm thick slices
4 zucchini (courgettes), cut on the diagonal into 2 cm thick slices
500 g pumpkin (squash), cut into 1.5 cm thick slices
basil leaves and a cherry tomato, to garnish (optional)

VINAIGRETTE

100 ml extra virgin olive oil
1 tablespoon finely chopped flat-leaf parsley
1 tablespoon finely chopped mint
2½ tablespoons good-quality balsamic vinegar
1 clove garlic, finely chopped
fresh or dried chilli, to taste (optional)
salt

To make the vinaigrette, mix the ingredients together in a small bowl with a spoon or fork.

Heat a barbecue grill plate to hot (use a heavy chargrill pan on the stove if you don't have a barbecue). Sprinkle the hot grill with a little salt, then add the sliced vegetables, one type at a time.

If you are including bell peppers, start with them as they tend to take the longest to cook. Next, grill the eggplant until it has brown stripes on one side, then turn over and cook the other side. Continue with the remaining vegetables – take care not to overcook them or they will taste too much of charcoal. When you have finished, arrange the vegetables on a serving plate and sprinkle with the vinaigrette. Garnish with basil leaves and a cherry tomato, if liked. Buon appetito!

NOTE *You can grill any other vegetables you like. I often include a couple of bell peppers, seeded and cut into small flattish pieces (peel off the charred skins before serving). Whole large mushrooms (flattened or sliced) are also good, as are wedges of juicy radicchio or fennel.*

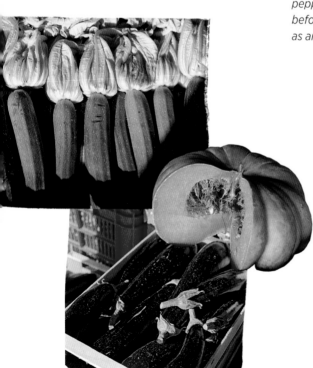

WITLOF WITH BEANS

CICORIE E FAGIOLI SECCHI

by Felice Fiore

This is an old Praiano recipe that used to be made with a locally grown salad green called 'sbrelle', which was very dark green and slightly bitter in taste. These days, witlof is commonly used, and its flavour is a perfect match for hearty borlotti beans. You'll need to soak the dried beans overnight so start Felice's classic recipe a day in advance.

SERVES 8

500 g dried borlotti beans
salt and pepper
pinch of bicarbonate of soda
120 ml extra virgin olive oil
2 cloves garlic, finely chopped
100 g pancetta, finely chopped
1 kg witlof (chicory), shredded
crusty bread, to serve (optional)

Soak the beans in plenty of water overnight, with a pinch of salt and bicarbonate of soda.

Drain the beans and place in a saucepan with fresh water and ½ teaspoon salt. Bring to the boil, then reduce the heat and cook, covered, for 30 minutes or until tender – they should not be al dente! Drain.

Heat the oil in a large heavy-based saucepan over medium heat, add the garlic, pancetta and witlof and cook, covered, for 10 minutes. Add the cooked beans and toss together for another 10 minutes. Season to taste and serve with crusty bread if liked.

NOTE *If they are in season, use shelled fresh beans instead.*

CONTORNI

This is yet another one of those incredibly simple but popular side dishes at Da Adolfo restaurant, where Daniele has ruled the kitchen for many years. The combination of fried potatoes and bell peppers doesn't really evoke seaside food, but it was so irresistible that it would finish before the lunch service even started. People would order it off the menu before they even sat down! This is so yummy I could happily eat a plate of it for lunch, with a good coffee to finish.

SERVES 4

750 ml peanut oil
600 g mixed yellow and red bell peppers, cut into 2 cm pieces
500 g pontiac potatoes, peeled, sliced and cut into 2 cm pieces
salt

Pour the oil into a medium heavy-based saucepan and heat over high heat until very hot but not smoking. Add the bell pepper pieces and cook until lightly golden, then scoop out with a slotted spoon and drain in a colander.

Reheat the oil and cook the potato until lightly golden. Remove with a slotted spoon and drain in the colander with the bell pepper.

Transfer the vegetables to a plate and season to taste with salt. This is best served hot, but you can also make it ahead of time and serve it at room temperature.

BELL PEPPERS AND POTATOES

PEPERONI E PATATE

by Daniele Bella

BLACK ANCHOVY AND WALNUT BREAD ROLLS

PANINI NERI CON ACCIUGHE E NOCI

by Valerio Buonocore

While I was researching Amalfi Coast recipes I learnt that walnuts and anchovies have always been presented together in this region. The combination goes back centuries – like shoes and socks, they're inseparable. You'll find them in pasta toppings, risottos, salads, sauces and even bread. Valerio created these sexy little black rolls and even won an award for them! The unusual addition of squid ink gives them the mystery they deserve.

MAKES ABOUT 50
35 g dried yeast
450 g strong plain flour (such as Italian '00')
665 g plain flour
300 ml pouring cream (or melted butter)
1 tablespoon honey
2 tablespoons squid ink
90 g eggs (1½ medium-sized eggs)
50 g walnuts, roughly chopped
80 g anchovies under olive oil or salt, rinsed well
　and roughly chopped
1 tablespoon salt

TOPPING
250 ml extra virgin olive oil
50 g walnuts
25 g anchovies

Dissolve the yeast in 100 ml water and set aside for a few minutes until frothy. If it does not start to froth, the yeast is dead and you will have to start again with a fresh batch.

Place the flours, cream, honey, squid ink, egg and 425 ml water in a large bowl, stir in the yeast mixture, then turn out onto a floured surface and knead for about 15 minutes or until smooth and elastic. Add the walnuts, anchovies and salt and knead until well combined. Return the dough to the bowl, cover with plastic film and leave to rise for 30 minutes.

On a well floured board or surface, roll out the dough to a thickness of 3 mm (it's easier if you also flour the top of the dough and the rolling pin). Cut out 4–5 cm rounds using a biscuit cutter or a glass, then cover with a clean tea towel and leave to rise for 35 minutes.

Preheat the oven to 200°C (fan-forced).

For the topping, brush the rounds with oil. Grind together the walnuts and anchovies in a mortar and pestle to make a rough paste, then smear over the rolls with your fingers, making little indents to decorate, if liked. Combine the remaining oil and paste in a small bowl.

Place the rounds on a large baking sheet, leaving about 3 cm between each one to allow for spreading, and bake on the middle shelf of the oven for 7–10 minutes or until risen and cooked through. Depending on the size of your oven, you may need to cook them in batches. Remove and cool on a wire rack. When cool, spoon a little more anchovy and walnut oil over the rolls.

NOTE *These amazing rolls make a meal in their own right when eaten straight from the oven with a hunk of cheese and a good drop of red!*

HOMEMADE BREAD PLAITS WITH PORK RIND AND PANCETTA

PANINI CON I CICCIOLI E PANCETTA

by Valerio Buonocore

This beautiful bread is made with pancetta and pork rind (no longer a poor man's food but a delicacy today). It has an amazing hearty flavour and will sit comfortably at any meal. My advice is to keep everything else very simple and let this powerhouse be the star of the show.

MAKES 30

30 g dried yeast
1.5 kg strong plain flour (such as Italian '00')
3 teaspoons sugar
75 g smoked pancetta, cut into 1 cm dice
75 g dried pork rind or ham skin, chopped into pieces
1¼ tablespoons salt
1 tablespoon ground pepper
about 60 whole almonds with skin

Dissolve the yeast in 100 ml cold water and set aside for a few minutes until frothy. If it does not start to froth, the yeast is dead and you will have to start again with a fresh batch.

Put the flour on a large clean surface and make a hole in the middle using a large flat spatula like Valerio's paddle (see page 53) or a regular spatula. Pour the yeast mixture into the hole and gradually knead the dough together with the sugar and 550 ml water Knead for 10–15 minutes or until it starts to form a dough. Add the pancetta, pork rind, salt and pepper and continue kneading until smooth and elastic. The dough is ready when you whack it and it sounds like a watermelon being slapped with the palm of your hand. Cover with plastic film and leave to rise for 20–30 minutes at warm room temperature.

Roll the dough into ropes about 20 cm long and 1 cm thick. Gently fold each rope in half so the ends are sitting side by side, then twist them together so it looks like a short fat plait. Press an almond into the space where you made the fold, and another after the first twist (see photo, right). Cover with a tea towel and leave to rise for another 45 minutes or until doubled in size.

Preheat the oven to 190°C (fan-forced). Place the dough plaits on large baking sheets and bake for 20 minutes or until cooked and golden. Keep an eye on them as all ovens have minds of their own and cooking times can vary quite significantly.

Anna TIZANI

NERANO, RESTAURANT OWNER

Anna is the very capable daughter of O'Re di Recommone (the King of Recommone beach), who started the family restaurant more than fifty years ago on this tiny cove tucked away on the Amalfi Coast. Anna and her three siblings now run this family business, which rocks all summer without pausing for breath. All four are great cooks but, as Anna says: 'Who has the time?'

Once upon a time, Anna's mother Giuseppina and her Uncle Vittorio ran the kitchen. Anna started working the restaurant floor when she was eleven and she's still going strong. The kitchen has since been taken over by a team of thirty experienced and well-selected chefs in crisp white garb, all under the watchful eye of Anna's sister Antonella, who checks every dish as it leaves the kitchen. She can see at a glance if the dish is up to scratch, which means the meals there are always mind-blowing.

Anna has the palate of a world-class food critic. She says it started when she was a child: clearing the guests' tables and taking the plates back to the kitchen, she'd often note that the 'best' bits were left on the plate. In those harder times, Anna would extract the sweet meat from the fine lobster claws or suck the cheeks from fish heads. Even then she could identify the finer flavours in life.

Anna grew up eating pesce all'acqua pazza (fish in crazy water; see page 194) and rabbit. One day her father had purchased two fat rabbits and stuck them on an abandoned island just opposite their little cove on the mainland, and so the family ate rabbit happily ever after! Her rabbit-riddled childhood has stuck, and she still prepares one of the most delicious rabbit dishes today (see page 159).

Anna, Antonella, Francesca and Orlando now run Conca del Sogno on the Amalfi Coast like a symphony orchestra: everyone has their instrument and Anna is the conductor. Her ambition is to run cooking schools around the world one day. She's already done so in Israel and at Harry's Bar in London – not a bad start. She'd love her next stop to be Australia – and so would I!

ANNA'S RECIPES

Anna's restaurant offers the most delicious antipasti imaginable on this coastline. Zucchini alla scapece is a classic recipe rarely left off a buffet table, and Anna's simple version is utterly delicious. She often serves it as a side dish with fish or meat.

SERVES 6

3 tablespoons extra virgin olive oil
2 tablespoons white wine vinegar
peanut oil, for frying
2 kg zucchini (courgettes), washed and cut
   on the diagonal into 5 mm thick slices
salt
2 cloves garlic, thinly sliced
1 teaspoon dried oregano
2 mint sprigs

Place the olive oil and vinegar in a small bowl and mix together with a spoon or fork. Set the dressing aside.

Pour the peanut oil into a heavy-based frying pan to a depth of at least 2 cm and heat until very hot but not smoking or burning. Add the zucchini slices in batches and cook until golden on both sides. Remove and drain well on paper towels.

While the zucchini slices are still warm, layer them on a serving platter and dress immediately – this way the dressing will be absorbed into the zucchini. Sprinkle with a little salt, then the garlic and oregano. Garnish with mint leaves.

NOTE *This can be prepared the day before but make sure the zucchini slices are well drained of excess oil. Bring to room temperature and dress just before serving.*

MARINATED FRIED ZUCCHINI

ZUCCHINI ALLA SCAPECE

by Anna Tizani

PRIMI

LINGUINE WITH FLYING SQUID

LINGUINE CON I TOTANI

by Vera Milano

This is one of the best seafood pasta dishes you can eat on the Amalfi Coast. As I have already mentioned, molluscs are either cooked for a long period of time or just very briefly – anything in between can give a tough and tasteless result. Vera has opted for light quick cooking in this fresh summer pasta and it is a triumph every time!

SERVES 6

2½ tablespoons extra virgin olive oil
½ white onion, finely chopped
2 cloves garlic, peeled and squashed
600 g red or plain squid, cleaned and cut into rings,
   tentacles chopped (ask your fishmonger to clean them for you)
12 cherry tomatoes, cut in half
salt and pepper
500 g linguine
roughly chopped flat-leaf parsley, to garnish
crusty bread, to serve (optional)

Heat the oil in a large frying pan over medium heat, add the onion and garlic cloves and cook until golden. Remove the garlic. Add the squid and tomatoes, increase the heat to high and cook for 5 minutes. Reduce the heat to medium and cook for another 10 minutes. Taste and season with salt and pepper if needed.

Meanwhile, cook the linguine in boiling salted water for 8 minutes or until al dente. Drain, reserving a cup of the cooking water. Add the linguine to the squid mixture and toss over medium heat for a minute, adding a little pasta water if the sauce is too thick. Sprinkle with parsley and serve immediately with tanto amore (and bread, if liked)!

ALWAYS USE A LARGE SAUCEPAN AND PLENTY OF WELL-SALTED WATER TO COOK PASTA. IT MUST BE BOILING FURIOUSLY BEFORE DROPPING IN THE PASTA, THEN COVER IMMEDIATELY WITH THE LID TO HELP THE WATER REGAIN ITS BOIL SO THE COOKING PROCESS IS AS CONSISTENT AS POSSIBLE.

SUPER PUMPKIN RISOTTO

ERIKA'S RISOTTO CON LA ZUCCA

by Erika Villani

One of the few vegetables that never really impressed me on the Amalfi Coast were the pumpkins. I'm sure it's because I've been thoroughly spoilt by the superb quality of Australian ones. So most of the Amalfi Coast recipes I've collected that use pumpkin have been prepared to get the absolute most out of their flavour. Erika's recipe may appear a little fussy but the end result is a thrilling risotto, crammed with flavour and texture, that can be prepared on a shoestring!

SERVES 4

1 tablespoon dried fennel
20 small pickling or cocktail onions
240 ml extra virgin olive oil, plus extra to serve
150 ml aged balsamic vinegar, plus extra to serve
salt
2 teaspoons sugar
1 clove garlic, peeled and left whole
1 kg sweet pumpkin (squash), cut into 1.5 cm dice
1 small white onion, finely chopped
200 g carnaroli rice
60 g parmesan, grated, plus extra to serve
30 g butter

Bring 2 litres water to the boil and add the dried fennel. Reduce the heat to very low and keep the fennel broth at a gentle simmer.

Bring another saucepan of water to the boil. Add the pickling or cocktail onions and cook for 1 minute to soften the skins. Drain, then remove a few layers of skin so they will be small and sweet.

Heat 120 ml oil in a small frying pan over medium heat, add the little onions and cook until they are nicely browned. Add 120 ml balsamic vinegar, 1 teaspoon salt and the sugar. Simmer for 5 minutes until the liquid has reduced and the smell of the vinegar has softened. Set aside.

Heat 3 tablespoons oil in a large frying pan over low heat, add the garlic clove and cook until golden. Remove the garlic. Add the pumpkin and cook, stirring, until tender. Take out half the pumpkin and puree in a blender. Set aside.

Heat the remaining oil in a large heavy-based saucepan over medium heat, add the chopped white onion and cook until transparent. Add the rice and half the diced pumpkin and mix for a minute, then add the remaining balsamic vinegar and simmer until it has evaporated. Increase the heat to high and add a ladleful of fennel broth. Stir until it has been absorbed into the rice before adding the next ladleful. Continue like this for 10 minutes, then stir in the pumpkin puree and cook for another 10 minutes, continuing to add the fennel broth, until the rice is al dente. Take the pan off the heat and add the parmesan and butter, stirring well until melted.

Spoon the risotto into four shallow bowls or use four ring moulds if you want to make it look extra special. Decorate with the pickling onions and remaining diced pumpkin. Finish with a few extra drops of balsamic vinegar and extra virgin olive oil and a sprinkling of parmesan.

NOTE *The cocktail onions and balsamic vinegar make this risotto quite sweet, which may not be to everybody's taste. If you like, leave them out and serve the risotto with crisp shards of grilled pancetta – the saltiness is a wonderful foil for the sweetness of the pumpkin.*

WHEN COOKING RISOTTO, MAKE SURE THE FLAME IS LIVELY OR THE RICE WILL TAKE TOO LONG TO ABSORB EACH LADLEFUL OF BROTH AND BECOME QUITE MUSHY. A GOOD RISOTTO SHOULD BE FIRM BUT CREAMY.

Erika VILLANI

MONTEPERTUSO, RESTAURANT OWNER AND CHEF

Erika cooks next to her mentor and mother Raffaela in their own little hilltop restaurant, Donna Rosa, perched above Positano in the minuscule town of Montepertuso (which means 'hole in the mountain' in dialect). This enormous mountain with its huge hole looms over the tiny piazza on which the family business sits.

But Erika has an unusual story. While Jamie Oliver was on his honeymoon, he visited Erika and Raffaella's little mountain retreat at the suggestion of his mentor, the great Amalfi Coast native and chef Gennaro Contaldo. Jamie was so impressed with Erika's homemade pasta that he immediately enlisted her to go to London and teach his enthusiastic students at the famous Fifteen restaurant.

Before that, another client who wandered into her restaurant was the famous Alain Ducasse. He immediately recognised Erika's natural flair for flavours in the kitchen and suggested that some formal technique would put her at the top of her game. He invited her to Monte Carlo, where he was teaching formal French cooking techniques to thirty-three capable young male French cooks. They were unforgiving and Erika often ended her days in frustrated tears, but like most tough tests in life it didn't kill her, it only made her better. Eventually she adapted her newly acquired skills to her kitchen on the mountain top and the result is one of the finest little eateries in Campania.

When you walk into Erika's restaurant, the first thing that hits you is the gentle feminine spirit of her world: with her Mama by her side in the kitchen and her multilingual sister working the floor, you can feel Aphrodite everywhere. But Papa Vincenzo fits in harmoniously as an excellent sommelier, gently suggesting the best wines for your meal.

Throughout the year, Erika offers hands-on cooking workshops. Her desire is to have her own little restaurant and continue to grow as an excellent chef, so she's exactly where she wants to be right now. She's the most capable and talented princess-cum-chef I've ever met!

ERIKA'S RECIPES

MASSIMO (STANDING) WITH BROTHER GIGI

Massimo PROTO

MAIORI, RESTAURANT OWNER AND CHEF

I met Massimo, one of the happiest and most dedicated foodies on the Amalfi Coast, more than five years ago while researching my first book, *My Amalfi Coast*. When visiting the wonderful Roman ruins in the tiny village of Minori one day, I happened upon Massimo's restaurant Arsenale and went in for a quick bite to eat. We got talking about my book and he immediately invited me into his kitchen to watch him prepare one the region's oldest pasta recipes (dating back hundreds of years), n'dunderi (see page 120). Massimo scored a double-page spread in *My Amalfi Coast* and became a good friend, introducing me to his three restaurateur brothers who helped run this eatery in their home town.

The four Proto brothers have since moved on and now run the very upmarket Torre Normanna restaurant in the slightly larger neighbouring town of Maiori, just one smooth curve down the Amalfi Drive away. Massimo and his cherished older brother Gigi still work the pots and pans together while Ivan and Daniele work the floor. Although Massimo has replaced his easy white T-shirt with a tall chef's hat and crisp coat with epaulets, his food is as true as ever.

When the Proto boys were growing up, their father was a wine and lemon trader, and this is how Massimo's passion for food started. Today the family still produces a boutique wine in nearby Ravello, which supplies the restaurant with a couple of hundred bottles of red and white each year.

Massimo enjoys his young family and house in Conca dei Marini down the coast. 'It's always a good thing to live and work in different villages on this coast,' Massimo says, 'or life can become very insular.' His passion is teaching people how to cook with the wonderful produce of the Amalfi Coast, which he somehow manages to squeeze into his very busy schedule.

Massimo's favourite dish to prepare is any pesce azzurro (deepwater fish such as tuna) and his favourite food to eat is the simple spaghetti aglio e olio. So often these incredibly capable and sophisticated chefs prefer the simplest of simple dishes. I dream of the day when I can sit on one of the old Tower's rocks down by the sea and eat a plate of aglio e olio with Massimo.

MASSIMO'S RECIPES

This popular pasta dish is exquisite in its simplicity. It sounds like making it should be child's play but having lived in Italy for over 20 years, I can safely say 'good' pasta aglio e olio is hard to come by. However, there are a couple of tricks: keep the heat low when cooking the garlic so it doesn't burn (Massimo finely slices his rather than finely chopping it so it doesn't burn as easily and holds it flavour better); and use good-quality Campania pasta if possible. The spaghetti is the main ingredient and should be the best.

SERVES 6

600 g good-quality spaghetti
150 ml extra virgin olive oil
4 cloves garlic, thinly sliced (preferably on a mandolin)
1 hot chilli, thinly sliced (or to taste)
1 anchovy under oil or salt, rinsed well (optional)
finely chopped flat-leaf parsley (to taste), plus extra leaves to garnish

Cook the spaghetti in boiling salted water for 8–10 minutes or until very al dente. Drain, reserving a cup of the cooking water.

Meanwhile, heat the oil in a large frying pan over low heat, add the garlic, chilli and anchovy (if using) and cook until the garlic is lightly golden and the anchovy has melted into the oil.

Add the spaghetti to the frying pan. Increase the heat to high and toss several times until the pasta is well coated in the oil, adding a spoonful or two of the pasta water. Take the pan off the heat and add plenty of parsley. Serve immediately, garnished with extra parsley leaves.

SPAGHETTI WITH GARLIC AND OIL

SPAGHETTI AGLIO E OLIO

by Massimo Proto

A TYPICAL ITALIAN WAY OF EATING THIS PASTA IS IN THE WEE HOURS OF THE MORNING, HOURS AFTER AN ENORMOUS MEAL AND MANY GLASSES OF GOD'S NECTAR. SOMEONE WILL SLIP AWAY TO THE KITCHEN AND REAPPEAR WITH A LARGE STEAMING BOWL OF PASTA AGLIO E OLIO. I WAS NEVER QUITE SURE IF THIS WAS TO HELP SOAK UP THE NECTAR OR JUST TOP OFF THE OVER-INDULGENCE — EITHER WAY, I HAPPILY DEVOURED EVERY STRAND !

BEAN SOUP

ZUPPA DI FAGIOLI

by Anna Tizani

This is a classic Italian recipe and most regions have their own take on it. I've prepared Adolfo's simple hearty version for decades with enormous success, and was fascinated to discover that Anna's slightly more complicated recipe is just as delicious but perhaps more interesting in texture due to the inclusion of silverbeet and scarola. The fiddly bits of this recipe are well worth it!

SERVES 4

250 g dried cannellini beans
2 tablespoons extra virgin olive oil, plus extra for drizzling
2 small white onions, chopped
2 small carrots, finely chopped
3 sticks celery, finely chopped
400 g silverbeet (Swiss chard), well washed and roughly chopped
400 g scarola or green endive, well washed and roughly chopped
2 small potatoes, peeled and roughly chopped
2 good-quality canned Italian tomatoes, drained, seeded and chopped
salt and pepper
fresh or dried chilli, to taste (optional)
toasted ciabatta croutons, to serve (optional)

Soak the beans in plenty of warm water overnight (not too hot). Drain the beans and place in a large heavy-based saucepan with enough fresh water to just cover the beans. Bring to the boil, then reduce the heat to low and cook, covered, for 2 hours or until tender. Check the water levels occasionally and top up with a little more hot water if needed. Drain.

Remove a quarter of the beans and set aside for later. Transfer the remaining beans to a blender and blend until smooth.

Heat the oil in a large heavy-based saucepan over medium heat, add the onion and cook until golden. Add the carrot, celery, silverbeet, scarola, potato and tomatoes and cook, stirring, for 15 minutes.

Add the pureed beans and enough water to cover all the vegetables. Season to taste with salt, pepper and chilli, if liked, then cook covered for 1 hour.

Stir in the reserved whole beans, then pour the soup into a well-heated soup terrine and drizzle with 2–3 tablespoons oil. If you like, serve with toasted croutons.

NOTE *You can serve this soup immediately if you like, but it tastes so much better the next day, once the flavours have had a chance to settle.*

LINGUINE WITH ROCK FISH

PASTA CON PESCE DI SCOGLIO

by Mario Rispoli

Every time I eat at Mario's little trattoria perched on a sloping sidewalk of Positano overlooking the Mediterranean sea, I really do try to order something different. But I cannot get past this simple yet astonishingly good pasta dish. The rock fish he uses in the sauce is the key: it is a bottom feeder and has more flavour than a trawler full of fresh prawns!

SERVES 6

100 ml extra virgin olive oil
2 cloves garlic, finely chopped
½ hot chilli, finely chopped
600 g cherry tomatoes, cut in half
600 g good rock fish (such as scorpion or turbot),
    filleted into 6 pieces
3 tablespoons white wine
500 ml fish stock (preferably homemade, see note below)
600 g linguine
finely chopped flat-leaf parsley, to garnish

Heat the oil in a large deep frying pan over medium heat, add the garlic and chilli and cook until the garlic is golden. Add the cherry tomatoes and cook for 10 minutes, then add the fish and wine and simmer for 5 minutes or until the wine has evaporated. Pour in the fish stock and cook for another 8 minutes or until the stock has mostly evaporated – turn the heat up to high for the last few seconds if needed.

Meanwhile, cook the linguine in boiling salted water for 8 minutes or until al dente. Drain the pasta, reserving a cup of the cooking water in case you need it for the sauce.

Just before the pasta is ready, squash a few pieces of fish in the pan with a fork and mix well into the sauce. Add the pasta and toss well for 1 minute over high heat. Add some of the reserved pasta water if the mixture is too dry. Sprinkle with parsley and serve hot.

NOTE *You must use linguine for this recipe. For some reason, it doesn't taste nearly as good with spaghetti, and you can completely forget about short pasta like tubetti or penne!*

FISH STOCK *You will get far superior results if you make your own fish stock. To do this, boil up fish heads, bones, prawn shells, bits of calamari – whatever you have to hand – in 1 litre of water for about 20 minutes. Strain through fine-meshed sieve and you're ready to go.*

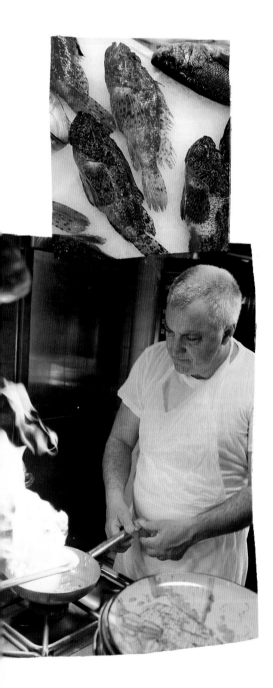

SPAGHETTI WITH MUSSELS IN RED SAUCE

SPAGHETTI CON LE COZZE IN ROSSO

by Daniele Bella

Ever since he was a kid, Daniele has been a master at preparing mussels. He used to take the big netted bags of mussels bought fresh every morning and tie them underwater at the end of the jetty – the movement of the waves would keep them open and flush out any impurities. In twenty years at Da Adolfo's restaurant, I never saw a bad mussel or a queasy customer! The tip here is to use screamingly fresh mussels, well bearded, scrubbed and plump. And ALWAYS discard the ones that just don't want to open. There's a reason for this: they're dead.

SERVES 4

1 kg mussels, cleaned and debearded
400 g spaghetti
100 ml extra virgin olive oil
2 cloves garlic, finely chopped
250 g cherry tomatoes, cut in half
small handful of flat-leaf parsley, finely chopped,
    plus extra sprigs to garnish (optional)

Bring 100 ml water to the boil in a large saucepan, add the mussels and cook, covered, until they open. As soon as they are open, remove the pan from the heat and let the mussels cool (if one or two don't open, just discard them). Take the mussels out of their shells and put in a bowl with the cooking liquid. (You can leave a few in the shell for decoration, if liked.)

Cook the spaghetti in boiling salted water for 8–10 minutes or until al dente. Drain, reserving a cup of the cooking water.

Meanwhile, heat the oil in a heavy-based frying pan over medium heat, add the garlic and cook until golden. Add mussels and tomatoes, then increase the heat to high and cook for 3 minutes. Pour in 100 ml of the mussel water and simmer until reduced to a creamy consistency.

Add the spaghetti to the mussel sauce and toss over high heat for 1 minute. If the dish looks too dry, add some of the pasta water. Toss through the chopped parsley and serve very hot garnished with extra parsley sprigs, if liked.

PENNE WITH FRESH TOMATO AND MOZZARELLA TOPPING

PENNE PRIMAVERA

by Daniele Bella

This fresh summer combination was invented by Daniele's father Adolfo, and was a favourite at his restaurant for decades. The idea is so simple: a Caprese salad of extra virgin olive oil, creamy mozzarella, juicy tomato and fresh basil on a steaming bowl of pasta. Just delicious! As is always the case with simple recipes, there is nowhere to hide so your ingredients must be in season and super fresh.

SERVES 6

300 g fresh mozzarella (preferably buffalo), cut into 1 cm dice
400 g tomatoes (preferably oxheart), cut into 1.5 cm dice
150 ml extra virgin olive oil
12 basil leaves, torn, plus 6 whole leaves to garnish
good pinch of oregano leaves
salt
500 g penne

Mix together the mozzarella, tomato, oil, torn basil, oregano and salt in a large bowl.

Meanwhile, cook the penne in boiling salted water for 8–10 minutes or until al dente. Drain, reserving a cup of the cooking water.

Toss the penne through the mozzarella mixture, adding a little pasta water if needed, and serve immediately, garnished with basil leaves.

NOTE *You can prepare the Caprese mixture a little in advance as the tomatoes will bleed a little juice which will add to the pasta topping – but be careful. If you prepare it more than half an hour ahead, the tomatoes will bleed out all of their juice and become flavourless.*

Daniele BELLA

POSITANO, CHEF BASED IN NEW SOUTH WALES

Daniele is a great chef and my son Marco's uncle. When Marco was tiny he'd jump up on a stool to help Zio impastare (uncle mix the dough) for whatever pie he was preparing for lunch that day. I had dreams for Marco's future as a great cook, but that was soon under threat from a soccer ball, a surfboard and girls.

Daniele is totally original and was the longest serving cook at Da Adolfo restaurant in Positano. Today he still cooks by feel and appears to work on roller skates in the kitchen, flying from one pan to other, grabbing ingredients on the way by the handful. He does little weighing or measuring but it all works fantastically. Despite his years of training as a pastry chef and his great love of all sweet things, his talent with savoury dishes has grown over the decades and they shot him to stardom as Da Adolfo's best chef in forty-five years. I've tried spaghetti con le cozze (spaghetti with mussels) up and down the Italian coastline for decades, but nobody can make it like Daniele, and his gateau di patate (potato bake) is so loved by the public that it makes children *cry* if it's not on the menu.

Luckily he's given me many of his recipes over the years, all of which I've carefully tested, measured and weighed. How else could I get it right?

Now living with his wife and children in the Southern Highlands near Sydney, Daniele is sorely missed on the Amalfi Coast, but on his annual visits he'll sometimes throw himself into the Da Adolfo kitchen and whip up a feast for his fan club. On the other hand, we pray for the day he opens his kitchen doors to indulge us with his long-awaited cooking classes in Australia. I can't wait! To check whether they're up and running, email book@amandatabberer.com.

DANIELE'S RECIPES

RAVOLI WITH PROVOLA AND EGGPLANT

RAVIOLI CON PROVOLA E MELANZANE

by Ada D'Urzo

This magnificent dish can be a little fiddly, but don't be put off. Once you have your tomato and bechamel sauces ready, all you need to do is prepare the pasta and filling and shape it into fat pillows. Ada generally serves just four or five of these monster ravioli drenched in the delicious tomato sauce. It's an amazing experience.

SERVES 6
basil leaves, to garnish
grated parmesan, to serve (optional)

TOMATO SAUCE
4 tablespoons extra virgin olive oil
1 clove garlic, peeled and left whole
1 kg cherry tomatoes, roughly chopped
salt

BECHAMEL SAUCE
50 g butter
100 g plain flour
500 ml milk
salt

PROVOLA AND EGGPLANT FILLING
2 medium eggplants (aubergines), cut into small dice
salt
250 ml peanut oil
250 g smoked provola cheese, cut into small dice
1 tablespoon grated parmesan
1 egg, lightly beaten

RAVIOLI DOUGH
1 kg strong plain flour (such as Italian '00')
400 ml boiling water
2½ tablespoons extra virgin olive oil
¼ teaspoon salt

To make the tomato sauce, heat the oil in a large saucepan over low heat. Add the garlic and cook until golden, then remove from the pan. Add the cherry tomatoes with a sprinkle of salt and cook over medium–high heat for 10–15 minutes until collapsed but still sweet and juicy. Take care not to overcook them, and if they start to dry out, add a little hot water. Set aside.

For the bechamel, melt the butter in a small saucepan over medium–low heat. Add the flour a little at a time, stirring vigorously to eliminate any lumps. Gradually pour in the milk, stirring constantly to stop any lumps forming. When the sauce is nice and thick, remove the pan from the heat, taste and season with salt if needed, then set aside.

To make the filling, place the eggplant in a colander, sprinkle with salt and leave for 30 minutes. Rinse well, then squeeze out any excess water with your hands. Pour the peanut oil into a large frying pan and heat until very hot but not smoking. Add the eggplant and cook until golden, then remove and drain on paper towels. Place the eggplant in a bowl with the provola, parmesan, egg and bechamel sauce and mix well.

For the ravioli dough, combine all the ingredients in a large bowl, then turn out onto a floured surface and knead until smooth – this should take 2 minutes. Divide the dough into two portions, then roll out one portion on a well-floured surface to a thickness of about 2.5 mm.

Roll tablespoons of the filling mixture into balls and place on the pasta sheet spaced evenly apart to create the ravioli size you would like. Do not make the balls too small or the ravioli will be doughy!

Roll out the second portion of dough to match the size of the first, then carefully place over the pasta sheet and filling. Using a 7–8 cm glass or biscuit cutter, cut out each ravioli with the filling in the centre. A blunt-edged glass is the best as it cuts the soft dough and seals each ravioli at the same time; if the ravioli are not sealed, gently press them closed with a fork or with your fingers.

Bring 2 litres water to the boil in a large saucepan and add plenty of salt. Carefully drop in the ravioli and cook for 10 minutes or until al dente. Remove with a slotted spoon and shake them gently to drain.

While the pasta is cooking, gently reheat the tomato sauce.

Divide the ravioli among serving plates or bowls, spoon the sauce over the top and decorate with basil leaves. Parmesan is optional as it is already in the filling.

SPAGHETTI OF THE CONVENT

SPAGHETTI ALLA CONVENTUALE

by Giuliano Donatantonio

Traditionally, this was made with whatever was available at the convent when the monks were hungry! Known as 'piatti poveri' (poor or simple dishes), the recipe is based on dried sheep's cheese and anchovies, as even the poorest households had a small supply of these in the kitchen. Giuliano has dozens of these dishes in his repertoire and always produces them lovingly and effortlessly for whoever happens to be at his table.

SERVES 4

4 tablespoons extra virgin olive oil
2 cloves garlic, finely chopped
8 anchovies under olive oil or salt, rinsed well
1 hot chilli, chopped
large handful of flat-leaf parsley leaves, finely chopped
500 g thick spaghetti
10 fresh walnuts, chopped, plus extra walnut halves to garnish (optional)
1 tablespoon grated pecorino
1 tablespoon fresh breadcrumbs made from stale bread (see page 30)
salt

Heat the oil in a large frying pan over medium heat, add the garlic and cook until golden. Add the anchovies, chilli and parsley and cook for about 3 minutes or until the anchovies start to melt into the oil. Remove the pan from the heat.

Meanwhile, cook the spaghetti in boiling salted water for 10 minutes or until al dente. Drain, reserving a cup of the cooking water.

Add the spaghetti to the anchovy mixture, along with the walnuts, pecorino and breadcrumbs, and toss together over high heat. Add some of the reserved pasta water to create a thick, creamy sauce. Garnish with extra walnut halves, if liked, and serve hot.

SPAGHETTI WITH SHELLFISH

SPAGHETTI CON I CROSTACEI

by Pasquale Marino

Pasquale first cooked this for me during a visit to Sydney a few years ago. He discovered the little blue swimmer crab at the fish markets and immediately envisaged a delicious bowl of Praiano pasta with an Aussie twist. We were entertaining a real-life Italian princess that evening, but when she was presented with this plate of magnificent shellfish atop a pile of pasta she didn't know where to start. Darling Pasquale quickly understood the princess's predicament, removed her plate and returned minutes later with completely de-shelled crab pasta!

SERVES 6

4 tablespoons extra virgin olive oil
2 cloves garlic, peeled and left whole
1 leek, white part only, washed and thinly sliced
2 hot chillies, sliced
3 large or 6 small blue swimmer crabs, split into quarters
   or halves if they are small (your fishmonger will do this
   for you – you don't need the top shell or the crab's back)
800 g cherry tomatoes, cut in half (use oxheart tomatoes
   if you prefer a less sweet sauce)
150 ml dry white wine
500 g spaghetti
flat-leaf parsley leaves, to garnish

Heat the oil in a large heavy-based frying pan over medium heat, add the garlic cloves, leek and chilli and cook until the garlic is golden. Remove the garlic.

Add the crab pieces, meat-side down, then cover and cook for 5 minutes. Add the tomatoes and cook uncovered for 10 minutes. Pour in the white wine and cook over medium–low heat for another 15 minutes.

Meanwhile, cook the spaghetti in boiling salted water for 8–10 minutes or until just al dente. Drain, reserving a cup of the cooking water.

Remove the crab pieces from the pan and toss the spaghetti through the tomato sauce, adding some of the reserved pasta water if necessary. Divide the spaghetti and sauce among serving plates and arrange the crab pieces on top. Finish with a garnish of parsley leaves.

If your crabs are small and delicate, you won't need any extra utensils to eat this dish, but if they are the larger ones you could probably do with some claw crackers to get the delicate meat out of the claws. Either way, wear a big bib!

THIS DISH IS NOT FOR THE FAINT-HEARTED AND YES THERE IS A LITTLE WORK INVOLVED TO EAT IT BUT IT IS WORTH IT! PRAIANO, PASQUALE'S VILLAGE, BOASTS MORE FISHERMEN THAN THE BAY OF NAPLES. EVERYONE FISHES AT SOME STAGE OF THEIR LIFE AND, CONSEQUENTLY, SOMETHING FROM THE SEA WILL ALWAYS END UP ON THE TABLE AT MEALTIMES. PASQUALE HAS COOKED THIS RECIPE FOR MANY YEARS WITH DIFFERENT CRUSTACEANS AND HE SAYS THAT THE BLUE SWIMMER IS A WINNER!

With its hearty chunks of eggplant and flavoursome pecorino, this is one of my favourite gnocchi dishes. I loved to eat it on rainy summer days when our beach restaurant was closed – we would hunker down at the little trattoria where Aldo has worked for years, cradling steaming bowls of this wonderfully comforting dish.

GNOCCHI WITH AGED PECORINO AND EGGPLANT

GNOCCHI AL PECORINO PICCANTE con MELANZANE

by Aldo Caso

SERVES 4

3 medium eggplant (aubergines), peeled and cut into 1.5 cm dice
50 g salt
500 ml peanut oil
2½ tablespoons extra virgin olive oil
1 clove garlic, peeled and left whole
1 kg good canned Italian tomatoes
large handful of basil leaves, plus extra to garnish
100 g chilli or pepper pecorino, cut or broken into small pieces
grated parmesan, to serve

GNOCCHI

500 g pontiac potatoes
150 g strong plain flour (such as Italian '00')
50 g parmesan, grated
1 teaspoon extra virgin olive oil
pinch of freshly grated nutmeg
pepper
100 g sea salt

Place the eggplant in a bowl, sprinkle with the salt and cover with cold water. Leave to soak for 15 minutes, then drain, squeeze dry and pat with paper towels. Heat the peanut oil in a large frying pan over medium heat until hot but not smoking, then add the eggplant and cook for 3–5 minutes until golden. Remove with a slotted spoon and drain on paper towels.

Heat the olive oil in a large frying pan over low heat, add the garlic clove and cook until golden. Remove the garlic. Add the canned tomatoes and cook for 20 minutes, then stir in the basil and eggplant. Just before serving, add the pecorino and stir for 1 minute or until the cheese has melted.

To make the gnocchi, boil the potatoes in their skins until tender. Drain and leave to cool slightly, then peel and press through a ricer while still hot. Set aside to cool completely. (If the pureed potato is warm the gnocchi dough will be too soft and you will have to add extra flour, which will make them rubbery and tough.)

Mix together the cold potato, flour, parmesan, oil, nutmeg and pepper to taste. Turn out onto a floured surface and knead until smooth and well combined. Roll the dough into ropes about 30 cm long and as thick as a cook's finger (Aldo's finger, not yours – cooks seem to have quite chunky fingers . . .) then cut them into 2 cm lengths.

Bring 5 litres water to the boil in a very large saucepan over high heat and add the sea salt. You have to add the gnocchi in small batches and keep the heat high so the water returns to the boil quickly; if you add all the gnocchi at once, the water will quickly lose its heat and the gnocchi will become a glug. The gnocchi are ready when they float to the surface. Quickly scoop them out with a slotted spoon, making sure the water is at a good boil, otherwise your gnocchi may still be raw inside. Drop the cooked gnocchi into a bowl of cold water while you cook the rest. Not only will this stop the cooking process, but also, if you add hot gnocchi directly to the sauce, they may dissolve. This way they hold their form.

When all the gnocchi are ready, drain them well and add to the hot sauce. Warm through, then serve immediately, garnished with extra basil leaves and grated parmesan.

CHESTNUT GNOCCHI

GNOCCHI DI CASTAGNA

by Giuseppe Francese

The town of Tramonti has always been known as the 'kitchen of the coast' – it's like one enormous larder, with its luscious natural produce lending an alternative touch to the usual 'fishy' menu offered in the seaside towns. The star of the show has to be the chestnut woodland which blooms around October. Chestnut season is celebrated with fabulous street festivals offering purees, cakes, gelati, sauces, flours, condiments, jams, chutneys and, naturally, delectable gnocchi! Here Giuseppe shares a true native's recipe.

SERVES 4

100 g fresh chestnuts
1 bay leaf
salt
20 g butter
100 ml pouring cream
1½ tablespoons milk
100 g caciotta or fresh ricotta, cut into small dice (see note below)
rosemary sprigs, to garnish

CHESTNUT GNOCCHI

500 g pontiac potatoes
100 g strong plain flour (such as Italian '00')
100 g chestnut flour
30 g parmesan, grated
1 egg
1 teaspoon salt

To make the chestnut gnocchi, boil the potatoes in their skins until tender. Drain and leave to cool slightly, then peel and press through a ricer while still hot. Spread on a flat surface (preferably marble or stone) and cool to warm room temperature. While still tepid, add the flours, parmesan, egg and salt and mix together. Don't overwork the dough or the gnocchi will be rubbery. On a floured surface, roll out the dough into ropes about 2 cm thick, sprinkling with flour as you go, then cut into 2 cm lengths.

Peel the hard outer layer off the chestnuts. Bring a large saucepan of water to the boil, add the bay leaf and some salt and cook the chestnuts for 40 minutes. Drain and cool slightly, then peel off the second, finer skin and chop into 1 cm pieces. Melt the butter in a medium saucepan over medium-low heat, then add the chestnut, cream, milk and caciotta or ricotta and cook for about 5 minutes until well combined – you are looking for a slightly thick but fluid consistency.

Meanwhile, bring a large saucepan of salted water to the boil. Drop in the gnocchi gently and slowly (trying not to lose the boil of the water) and scoop them out with a slotted spoon as soon as they rise to the surface. Add to the chestnut sauce and cook briefly and gently until well combined. Add a little gnocchi cooking water if the sauce is too thick. Serve hot, garnished with a sprig of rosemary.

NOTE *Caciotta is a fresh soft cheese made from cow's or sheep's milk. Look for it in specialty food stores, select delis and cheese shops.*

SPAGHETTI WITH CHERRY TOMATOES, ANCHOVIES, PINE NUTS AND SULTANAS

SPAGHETTI CON POMODORINO, ACCIUGHE, PINOLI E SULTANINE

by Gennaro Marciante

Cetara functions with little tourism and lots of fish, being the only surviving fishing village on the Amalfi Coast. Gennaro is a true Cetara native and outstandingly clever at using the wonderful flavours from the sea. Anchovies have always been one of Cetara's main produce, but if you can't obtain Cetara anchovies, use good-quality ones packed under salt or bottled in extra virgin olive oil. Nothing else, otherwise the entire flavour of the dish will be wrong.

SERVES 6

500 g spaghetti (see note below)
3 tablespoons extra virgin olive oil
1 clove garlic, peeled and squashed
12 cherry tomatoes, cut in half
100 g pine nuts
100 g sultanas
2 anchovies under olive oil or salt, rinsed well
salt
120 g parmesan, grated
2 tablespoons finely chopped flat-leaf parsley
6 basil leaves, torn

Cook the spaghetti in boiling salted water for 8 minutes or until al dente. Drain, reserving a cup of the cooking water.

Meanwhile, heat the oil in a large frying pan over low heat, add the garlic clove and cook until golden. Remove the garlic. Add the tomatoes and cook until they start to collapse, then add the pine nuts, sultanas and anchovies and cook for 2 minutes. Add a little of the pasta water if the mix is too dry, then season to taste with salt.

Add the pasta to the tomato mixture and toss together for a minute. Add a little more pasta water if necessary, then remove from the heat and sprinkle over the parmesan, parsley and basil. Toss again and serve immediately.

NOTE *To get the most out of this simple dish, use top-quality spaghetti, preferably artisan or 'bronzed'. And check the instructions on the packet – you want the thickness that takes 8 minutes to cook.*

This can be one hell of a messy dish to prepare if you are not organised. But don't be put off – this stunning dish is worth a little effort. Like her mama Raffaela, Erika has a great talent for making pasta, and this is one of her best recipes. The apple doesn't fall far from the tree in Italian kitchens.

SERVES 4
90 ml extra virgin olive oil
1 clove garlic, finely chopped
16 anchovies under olive oil or salt, rinsed well,
    plus extra to garnish (optional)
300 g cherry tomatoes, cut in half
wild rocket, to serve
fresh or dried chilli, to serve
2 tablespoons finely chopped flat-leaf parsley

TAGLIATELLE DOUGH
200 g durum wheat flour, plus extra if needed
100 g strong plain flour (such as Italian '00')
1 heaped teaspoon salt
3 eggs
3½ tablespoons squid ink, plus extra if needed

To make the tagliatelle dough, place the flours and salt on a clean surface and make a well in the middle. Pour the eggs and squid ink into the well and mix together, starting with a fork and eventually, when the dough starts to come together in a ball, knead with the heel of the hand. To clean the black ink off your hands, don't wear gloves! Just sprinkle your hands with flour and rub them over the pasta ball until the ink wears off. If the dough is not dark enough, add more squid ink until you reach the desired depth of colour. Knead the dough with light, fast fingers for about 10 minutes or until nice and compact. If it appears a little sticky, add small amounts of durum wheat flour until you get a decent consistency.

Cut the dough ball in half. Roll out one ball on a floured surface to a thickness of about 2 mm. Brush off any excess flour with a pastry brush, then roll up the dough and cut into 5 mm-wide strips. Repeat with the remaining ball of dough.

Heat the oil in a large heavy-based saucepan over low heat, add the garlic and cook until lightly golden – don't let it burn! Add the anchovies and stir for a few seconds, then add the tomatoes. Increase the heat to high and cook the tomatoes for just 2 minutes so they remain 'alive', as the locals say. You don't want them to become sloppy like a tomato sauce.

Bring a large saucepan of water to the boil (at least 3 litres of water) and add a little salt – not too much as the anchovies in the sauce are already quite salty. Drop the tagliatelle into the boiling water and cook for 6 minutes or until still a little al dente. Drain, reserving a cup of the cooking water.

When the tagliatelle is nearly ready, gently reheat the sauce over medium heat. Add the drained tagliatelle and gently toss to combine for a minute or two so it finishes cooking and marries with the sauce. Remove from the heat. If the sauce is too thick add a spoonful of the reserved pasta water. Spoon into pasta bowls and top with rocket leaves and an anchovy fillet, if liked, then finish with a sprinkling of chilli and parsley.

If you want to make it extra special, spoon the pasta into hot serving rings, wait just long enough for the pasta to hold its form, then remove the rings, garnish and serve.

TAGLIATELLE WITH SQUID INK, ANCHOVIES, CHERRY TOMATOES AND WILD ROCKET

TAGLIATELLE AL NERO DI SEPPIA CON ALICI SALATE, POMODORINI E RUCOLA

by Erika Villani

ZUCCHINI SPAGHETTI

SPAGHETTI
CON I ZUCCHINI

by Rosetta D'Urso

Originally seen in the area of Nerano many decades ago, this dish has been interpreted by every cook on the coastline, including some of the best restaurants. But Rosetta's recipe stands out. Her trick? I believe it's the two different ways she prepares the zucchini before bringing them together, and her ample quantity of basil. Be generous: zucchini and basil are a match made in heaven!

SERVES 6

500 ml peanut oil
2 kg zucchini (courgettes), cut into 5 mm thick rounds
30 g butter
1½ tablespoons extra virgin olive oil
½ small onion, chopped
1 heaped tablespoon salt
200 ml thickened cream
100 g parmesan, grated
30 young and tender basil leaves
500 g spaghetti

Heat the peanut oil in a large deep frying pan over medium–high heat until hot but not smoking. Add half the zucchini and cook until golden. Remove with a slotted spoon and drain in a colander.

Combine the butter and olive oil in a large saucepan over low heat until the butter has melted. Add the onion and cook until transparent. Add the remaining zucchini, the salt and 125 ml water and cook gently for about 20 minutes. Remove the pan from the heat, then stir in the fried zucchini and set aside.

Roughly tear 10 basil leaves and combine in a large bowl with the cream and parmesan. Stir in the zucchini mixture.

Cook the spaghetti in boiling salted water for 7–8 minutes. Keep an eye on it as you want to remove it 2 minutes before it is ready. Drain, reserving a cup of the cooking water as you will need some for the sauce. This is very important as the zucchini paste can be dry.

Add the pasta and a little pasta water to the zucchini paste and toss until well mixed.

OR, using a pasta fork, you can fish the pasta out of the hot water directly into the bowl with the zucchini, which will automatically take some liquid with it, then toss everything together.

Divide the pasta among serving bowls and garnish with the remaining basil leaves. Eat immediately.

ROSETTA HAS BEEN COOKING THIS DISH FOR OVER 25 YEARS. I NAGGED ITS SECRET OUT OF HER WELL BEFORE CONSIDERING ITS INCLUSION IN A RECIPE BOOK, AND REALISE NOW THAT I HAVE BEEN COOKING IT FOR OVER 20 YEARS.

This is another fast-cooking mollusc recipe. Angela says it's just a matter of coordinating the separate pans and bringing it all together at the end for a mouth-watering result. This is a great example of a typical coastal dish using good-quality potatoes and pasta, with an added burst of flavour from the calamari.

SERVES 6

120 ml extra virgin olive oil
1 clove garlic, finely chopped
2 medium pontiac potatoes, cut into 1.5 cm dice
1 clove garlic, extra, peeled and left whole
½ hot chilli, finely chopped
pinch of pepper
4 medium calamari tubes, cleaned and cut into 1.5 cm dice
500 g small striped tubetti
8 basil leaves, ripped, plus extra to garnish

Heat 3 tablespoons oil in a large frying pan over low heat. Add the chopped garlic and cook until lightly coloured, then add the potato and cook, stirring, for 10 minutes or until golden and cooked through.

While the potato is cooking, heat 2 tablespoons oil in another frying pan over medium heat, add the whole garlic clove, chilli and pepper and cook until the garlic is golden. Remove the garlic. Add the calamari and cook for 5–7 minutes – any longer and it'll turn to rubber.

Meanwhile, cook the tubetti in boiling salted water for 10 minutes or until al dente.

Add the calamari to the potato. Toss over medium–low heat for 5 minutes, then add the basil leaves and remove from the heat.

Drain the pasta, reserving a cup of the cooking water, and toss through the calamari and potato mixture. Add some of the reserved pasta water if the mixture is too dry. Serve piping hot, garnished with extra basil leaves.

NOTE *It's important that you rip the basil leaves rather than cutting them, otherwise they'll take on the metallic flavour of the knife, killing the perfume. This applies to any fresh herb.*

TUBETTI PASTA WITH CALAMARI, POTATO AND BASIL

TUBETTI CON CALAMARI, PATATE E BASILICO

by Angela Giannullo

SPAGHETTI WITH GIANNI'S INCREDIBLE TOMATO SAUCE

SPAGHETTI CON POMODORO

by Gianni Irace

This is the most unlikely dish to get excited about, but the first time I ate it was while shooting *My Amalfi Coast* with Carla Coulson. It was late (even by Italian standards) but Gianni welcomed us with his usual happy smile. Seeing our exhausted faces, he offered us a nice simple pasta con pomodoro and a glass of chilled wine. I'd spent decades eating at Gianni's little restaurant and didn't think anything could surprise me, but we were in for such a treat: clean, simple, aromatic pasta cooked with love and passion. I'm sure Gianni whipped it up himself as the chef would have gone for the day. Carla and I were in heaven.

SERVES 6

100 ml extra virgin olive oil, plus extra to serve
1 clove garlic, peeled and squashed
4–5 large, ripe oxheart tomatoes, cut into 3 cm dice
5–6 basil leaves, torn, plus extra leaves to garnish
500 g medium-thick spaghetti
50 g parmesan, grated

Heat the oil in a large heavy-based frying pan over medium heat, add the garlic clove and cook until golden. Remove the garlic. Add the tomato and basil, increase the heat to medium–high and cook, stirring, for 10 minutes.

Meanwhile, cook the spaghetti in boiling salted water for 8–10 minutes or until very al dente. Drain, reserving a cup of the cooking water.

Toss the spaghetti through the sauce, adding some of the reserved pasta water if necessary. Just before removing the pan from the heat, add half the parmesan and mix quickly. Serve immediately with the remaining parmesan and a drizzle of oil, garnished with extra basil leaves.

THE POMODORO SORRENTINO (SORRENTO TOMATO OR OXHEART TO US) IS A BIG FLESHY, SWEET-TASTING TOMATO USED IN SALADS. THEY ALSO CALL IT 'POMODORO PER l'INSALATA' — TOMATOES FOR SALAD. IT IS NOT COMMON TO USE THEM IN COOKING BUT GIANNI DEVELOPED THIS DELICIOUS PASTA DISH (ABOVE) WHICH HAS A LIGHTNING BOLT OF FLAVOUR. ANGELA, ON THE FACING PAGE, GOES FOR A MORE CLASSIC STYLE WITH THE 'POMODORINO A PIENNOLO' — BUNCHED SMALL OVAL TOMATOES FAMOUS FOR THE AMAZING 'SEA' FLAVOUR THEY ACQUIRE GROWING BY THE SEASIDE.

This dish has a traditional story on the coast and although it's a very humble recipe, its ironic name tells of the sea flavour trapped inside the cherry tomatoes that grow in the sun by the sea. There is NO fish in this recipe but a wonderful hint of its aroma in the sauce! I cook this every week for friends and family; the trick is the flame under the pan when you throw in the tomatoes – it should be nice and lively. Angela has added her own signature by stirring in a touch of pesto at the end.

SERVES 6

120 ml extra virgin olive oil
1 clove garlic, peeled and left whole
1 kg sweet cherry tomatoes
1 tablespoon basil pesto (preferably homemade)
500 g spaghetti
grated parmesan, to serve

Heat the oil in a large heavy-based frying pan over medium heat, add the garlic clove and cook until golden. Remove the garlic. Increase the heat to high, add the tomatoes (gently as you will get a bit of spatter) and cook, stirring, for 8–10 minutes or until the sauce is orange and creamy. Stir in the pesto at the end.

Meanwhile, cook the spaghetti in boiling salted water for 8–10 minutes or until very al dente. Drain, reserving a cup of the cooking water.

Toss the spaghetti through the sauce, adding a spoonful of the reserved pasta water if necessary. Serve immediately with a sprinkling of parmesan.

SPAGHETTI WITH 'THE FISH THAT GOT AWAY'

SPAGHETTI CON PESC' FUIT'

by Angela Giannullo

WHEN COOKING CHERRY TOMATOES FOR A CREAMY TOMATO SAUCE, ALWAYS TOSS THEM ON A LIVELY FLAME. THIS GIVES THE SAUCE ITS GORGEOUS CREAMY ORANGE COLOUR AND LOCKS IN THE FLAVOURS. THIS SIMPLE SAUCE IS A GREAT BASE FOR ANY EXTRA INGREDIENTS YOU CHOOSE TO ADD.

LIKE MOST ITALIANS, THE NATIVES OF THE AMALFI COAST CONSIDER THEMSELVES TO BE GREAT ARTISTS. EVERYTHING FROM CERAMIC TILES AND MOSAIC PIAZZAS TO DECORATED MADONNAS AND HAND-PAINTED SIGNS HAVE BEEN PAINSTAKINGLY DESIGNED. THERE IS LITTLE GRAFFITI IN THIS NECK OF THE WOODS, SIMPLY BECAUSE THERE IS <u>NO</u> ROOM FOR IT!

ANGEL-HAIR PASTA WITH PRAWNS AND LEMON

CAPELLINI CON GAMBERI E LIMONE

by Gianni Irace

The use of cream suggests that this recipe is not traditional to this area, but Gianni's addition of this small hint of luxury has given the dish his signature of exquisite flavour. Gianni has been involved with food on the Amalfi Coast for so many decades and he is a natural at developing exciting fresh flavours. The coupling of cream and aromatic local lemons is inspired, but like all luxurious things – never too much.

SERVES 6

120 ml extra virgin olive oil
¼ white onion, very finely sliced
600 g peeled raw prawns (not too big), heads and tails intact (if liked)
1½ tablespoons vodka
2½ tablespoons thickened cream
finely grated zest of 1 lemon
500 g angel-hair pasta, broken into two or three pieces
50 g parmesan, grated
½ lemon

Heat the oil in a large saucepan over low heat, add the onion and cook gently until transparent. Add the prawns and cook for 1 minute, then pour in the vodka and toss for 30 seconds. Add the cream and half the lemon zest and cook for 2 minutes. Remove from the heat.

Cook the pasta in boiling salted water (with 2 drops of oil so they don't stick together) for 3 minutes or until al dente. Drain, reserving a cup of the cooking water.

Add the pasta to the prawns and toss for a few seconds, adding a little of the reserved pasta water if the sauce is too thick. Add the parmesan while tossing the pasta and sauce together.

Divide among shallow bowls or plates and sprinkle with the remaining lemon zest. Finish each serve with five drops of lemon juice.

NOTE *The trick with this dish is to work quickly. Al dente angel-hair pasta is delicious, but it only takes 3 minutes to cook so make sure all the other ingredients are prepared before you start.*

SCHIAFFONI WITH CUTTLEFISH ALLA SARACENA

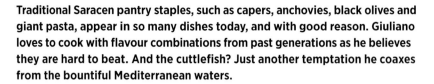

SCHIAFFONI CON SEPPIE ALLA SARACENA

by Giuliano Donatantonio

Traditional Saracen pantry staples, such as capers, anchovies, black olives and giant pasta, appear in so many dishes today, and with good reason. Giuliano loves to cook with flavour combinations from past generations as he believes they are hard to beat. And the cuttlefish? Just another temptation he coaxes from the bountiful Mediterranean waters.

SERVES 4

3 tablespoons extra virgin olive oil
2 cloves garlic, finely chopped
10 salted capers, rinsed and drained
1 hot chilli, finely chopped
2 anchovies under olive oil or salt, rinsed well
600 g cuttlefish, well cleaned, cuttlefish and tentacles sliced
3 tablespoons white wine
1 × 400 g can Italian tomatoes
10 black olives, pitted
salt
400 g schiaffoni
chopped flat-leaf parsley, to garnish

Heat the oil in a large heavy-based frying pan over medium heat, add the garlic, capers, chilli and anchovies and cook until the garlic is golden. Toss in the cuttlefish and white wine and simmer until the wine has evaporated. Pass the canned tomatoes through a ricer and add to the pan with the olives and small amount of salt (you don't need much because of the anchovies). Simmer, covered, for 30 minutes.

Meanwhile, cook the schiaffoni in boiling salted water for 15–20 minutes or until al dente. Drain, reserving a cup of the cooking water.

Add the pasta to the sauce and toss over high heat until combined, adding a little of the pasta water if the sauce is too thick. Sprinkle the parsley over the top and serve.

NOTE *Schiaffoni is giant pasta and is readily available at Italian grocers and delis.*

AS THE SARACENS CONSTANTLY INVADED THESE TEMPTING COASTAL VILLAGES, THERE BECAME CERTAIN PANTRY SUPPLIES THAT COULD NEVER BE DONE WITHOUT, SUCH AS THE KEY INGREDIENTS IN THIS RECIPE. ALL THINGS WITH A GOOD SHELF LIFE WERE HOARDED AS YOU NEVER KNEW WHEN YOU'D GET TO THE CORNER STORE AGAIN!

ROSETTA (LEFT) WITH SISTER-IN-LAW GRAZIELLA

Rosetta D'URSO

POSITANO, HAIRDRESSER

For decades Rosetta has spent her days styling and cutting hair as one of the main hairdressers in Positano, working on locals, tourists and many a bride. When my son, Marco, was three years old he was complimented on his golden locks and called a beautiful little girl one time too many. They had to go, and Rosetta did the deed for me. Funnily enough, his big butch dad was the most upset of all.

Despite her frantic daily schedule in the salon, Rosetta somehow finds time to produce delicious meals for family and friends. No matter what time of day I'd drop by, there'd always be something tasty to sample – an eggplant roll stuffed with mozzarella and fresh basil leaves, dripping in homemade tomato sauce; a mouth-watering lemon plum cake for afternoon tea; or even a stuffed baby squid sitting in solitary confinement on the top shelf of her fridge.

Her food passion started in her late teens when she worked in her uncle's trattoria down on the main beach of Positano, although she only waited tables in those days. Her coordination in the kitchen today is second to none; she often manages eight to ten different dishes simultaneously, definitely an influence from her early trattoria days – and all from a kitchen the size of a broom closet.

We often eat on her terrace, which acts as a second kitchen, among the flapping salon towels drying in the Mediterranean breeze. Rosetta has a stovetop close to the table so she can offer boiling-hot pasta dishes. 'Never eat pasta cold!' she says. In Italy the saying goes 'La pasta non aspetta (Pasta does not wait)'. In other words, forget decorum, don't wait for the others, just tuck in as soon as the bowl is in front of you.

Rosetta's recipes are a mix of traditions handed down by family members over the decades and her natural instinct for good flavours plus the joy of cooking for her loved ones, of which I'd like to think I'm one. She's been gracious enough to share some of them with me here. A meal cooked by Rosetta is definitely my first-stop destination every time I return to Positano.

ROSETTA'S RECIPES

This traditional dish always brings back fond memories. Years ago, we were driving through an unsavoury part of Castellammare when we spotted a three-wheeler van laden with so much cima di rapa (a local green also known as broccoli rabe or raab) we could barely make out the van. We chased after him, yelling out the window and scared the poor devil half to death! We only wanted to buy some broccoli but he obviously had other fears, which is quite justified in that part of town. In the end we bought half his load, grabbed some pork sausages on the way home and made this mouth-watering meal. It was a triumph, thanks to the old boy's broccoli!

ORECCHIETTE WITH BROCCOLI AND SAUSAGE

ORECCHIETTE CON BROCCOLI E SALSICCE

by Rosetta D'Urso

SERVES 4

400 g Italian pork sausages, preferably with fennel seeds
4 tablespoons extra virgin olive oil
2 cloves garlic, peeled and squashed
salt
½ hot chilli, finely chopped
1 kg young broccoli rabe leaves or any cookable bitter green,
    well washed, chopped if necessary
320 g orecchiette

Remove the sausage meat from the casings and break up into bite-sized pieces. Set aside.

Heat the oil in a large frying pan over medium heat oil, add the garlic and chilli and cook until golden – take care not to let it burn. Remove the garlic, then add the sausage bits and cook for 10 minutes.

Meanwhile, bring 2 litres water to the boil in a large saucepan. Add a generous pinch of salt, then drop in the broccoli and cook for 10 minutes or until tender. If the stems are thick, cook for a few minutes longer.

Cook the orecchiette in boiling salted water for 10–15 minutes or until al dente.

Meanwhile, drain the broccoli, reserving about a cup of the cooking water. Add the broccoli and reserved cooking water to the sausage meat and toss briefly over high heat to amalgamate. Drain the orecchiette and add to the pan. Toss briefly over high heat, then taste and season with a little more salt if needed. Serve immediately.

NOTES *Adolfo taught me a slightly different method. Prepare the sausage and broccoli in the same way, adding the cooked broccoli to the sausage in a large deep frying pan. Add about 500 ml of hot water, 1–2 teaspoons salt and bring everything to the boil. Add the orecchiette and cook over high heat, stirring frequently. Keep an eye on the liquid: if it thickens up too quickly, add a bit more boiling water; if it appears too liquid, take out some liquid with a ladle. When the orecchiette are ready you should have a creamy dish of sausage, broccoli and pasta.*

Whichever method you use, a sprinkle of grated parmesan is optional. And watch your tongue – it will be boiling hot! Eat with gusto.

GNOCCHI WITH TOMATO, MOZZARELLA AND BASIL

GNOCCHI ALLA SORRENTINA

Mena Vanacore

This is a favourite amongst the kids of the coast, but also appeals to adults who just want something clean and simple after too many extravagant flavours. Having said that, this classic dish is totally delicious and anything but simple – making fresh gnocchi is an art. Like the famous Delizia al limone (see page 204), it was born in nearby Sorrento and is savoured on every menu up and down the coast.

SERVES 6-8

1 tablespoon extra virgin olive oil
1 clove garlic, peeled and left whole
3 × 400 g cans Italian tomatoes
large handful of basil leaves, roughly torn
salt
½ teaspoon sugar (optional)
400 g mozzarella, cut into 2 cm dice
100 g parmesan, grated, plus extra to serve

GNOCCHI
1 kg pontiac potatoes
2 eggs
salt
400 g strong plain flour (such as Italian '00')

To make the gnocchi, boil the potatoes in their skins until tender. Drain and leave to cool slightly, then peel and press through a ricer while still hot. Pile the potato onto a flat surface and make a well in the middle. Break the eggs into the well and add a pinch of salt. Pour the flour around the potato. Gradually work the flour into the potato and egg mixture, working with swift, light fingers – do not overwork the dough or the gnocchi will be rubbery.

Roll the dough into ropes about 15 cm long and 1.5 cm thick, adding a small sprinkling of flour if they get sticky (not too much or they'll become tough). Cut into 1 cm lengths and gently press onto the tines of a fork to make tracks to trap the sauce.

Heat the oil in a large saucepan over low heat, add the garlic clove and cook until golden. Remove the garlic. Add the tomatoes, half the basil and a little salt. Bring to the boil over medium–high heat and cook for 30 minutes. Taste during cooking and if the tomatoes are a bit sour, add the sugar.

Preheat the oven to 200°C (fan-forced).

Bring 3 litres water to the boil in a very large saucepan over high heat and add 3 teaspoons salt. Add the gnocchi in small batches and boil until the gnocchi rise to the surface. Quickly scoop them out with a slotted spoon, making sure the water is at a good boil, otherwise your gnocchi may still be raw inside.

Place the well-drained gnocchi in a large baking dish and add the tomato sauce, mozzarella, parmesan and remaining basil. Mix lightly and well. If you want to make individual serves, spoon the mixture into small ovenproof dishes. Bake for 20 minutes or until the mozzarella has melted. Sprinkle a little extra parmesan over the top and serve. Watch your tongue with the first mouthful – it will be 'bolente' (boiling hot)!

STUFFED INVOLTINI OF BEEF WITH PASTA

LE BRACIOLE CON LA PASTA

by Carla Rispoli

This is one of the first dishes I tried when I moved to the Amalfi Coast and it took me completely by surprise. The combination of beef, pine nuts, sultanas and pecorino was an absolute revelation. Just the thought of it brings a tear to my eye – not to mention the delectable aromas as it bubbles away in the kitchen. I could chop down trees after eating a plate of this, and Carla's recipe is one of the best!

SERVES 6

6 slices sirloin fillet (ask your butcher to make them about 5 mm thick)
6 very thin slices of lardo (cured pork fat)
salt and pepper
1 clove garlic, finely chopped
60 pine nuts
30 sultanas
1 small bunch flat-leaf parsley, finely chopped
200 g pecorino romano, shaved
3 tablespoons extra virgin olive oil
2 cloves garlic, extra, peeled and squashed
1½ tablespoons white wine
2 × 400 g cans Italian tomatoes
500 g rigatoni
grated pecorino romano, extra, to serve

Spread the sirloin slices on a clean work surface, top each with a slice of lardo and sprinkle with salt and pepper.

Divide the chopped garlic, pine nuts, sultanas, parsley and pecorino evenly among the meat slices, then roll up tightly to enclose the filling. Secure the involtini with toothpicks.

Heat the oil in a deep frying pan large enough to hold all six involtini and the pasta. Add the squashed garlic cloves and cook over medium heat until golden. Remove the garlic, then add the involtini and cook until browned on all sides. Pour in the white wine and cook until it has evaporated.

Roughly chop the tomatoes with a long pointed knife while still in the can, then add to the pan. Rinse the cans with a small amount of water and add that as well. Season with salt, then cover and bring to a gentle boil. Reduce the heat to very low and cook for 2 hours with the lid slightly askew, checking regularly to make sure it does not dry out. Add a little water if the sauce is looking dry and move the involtini very delicately to help them cook evenly and stop them sticking to the pan.

Cook the rigatoni in boiling salted water for 10–12 minutes or until al dente. Drain, reserving a cup of the cooking water.

Remove the involtini from the tomato sauce, then tip the pasta into the sauce and stir until well combined.

Divide the pasta and involtini among six plates and finish with a sprinkling of grated pecorino.

BY THE WAY, BRACIOLE IS A LITTLE INVOLTINO BUT THIS WORD IN THIS PART OF ITALY REFERS TO THE LIFE-SAVING RINGS KIDS WEAR AROUND THEIR ARMS IN THE WATER. IT STILL WORKS THOUGH AS THESE EDIBLE ONES ARE ALSO A LIFE SAVER!

GIANT SPIRALS WITH BROAD BEANS AND PANCETTA

Local friends would deliver beautiful young broad beans to our beach restaurant weeks before we even opened, and we would devour this pasta dish in the middle of the construction chaos. One year, my brother Nico was visiting and gatecrashed one of these lunches, and for years afterwards he would beg me to make it for him. He swore it was one of the best meals he'd ever had!

SERVES 4

70 ml extra virgin olive oil
300 g cleaned young broad beans (the smaller the better)
50 g Italian pancetta (not bacon), cut into 5 mm dice
½ small onion, finely chopped
350 g fusilli
salt
70 g parmesan, grated, plus extra to garnish

Heat the oil in a heavy-based frying pan over medium–high heat, add the broad beans and pancetta and cook for 5–10 minutes until the beans are golden. Add the onion and cook for a further 3–4 minutes.

Meanwhile, cook the fusilli in boiling salted water for 8–12 minutes or until al dente.

Add a cup of the boiling pasta water to the broad bean mixture, season generously with salt and cook for another 5 minutes.

Drain the fusilli, reserving some of the cooking water. Add the pasta to the broad bean mix and toss together for 1 minute. Add a little more pasta water if the sauce is looking dry – this will also make the sauce a bit creamier. Stir in the parmesan and serve with a little extra parmesean sprinkled over the top. Buon appetito!

NOTE *The best broad beans are in season in southern Italy just before summer. You want the smaller, sweeter ones that are good to eat with their skins straight from the pod, not the big woody guys that need peeling.*

GIANT SPIRALS WITH BROAD BEANS AND PANCETTA

FUSILLI GIGANTI con LE FAVE e PANCETTA

by Daniele Bella

This is a simple peasant dish with a lot of passion. It's a classic, sure to make any good Neapolitan living abroad yearn for home.

SERVES 6-8

500 g pontiac potatoes, peeled and cut into 2 cm cubes
salt
600 g small striped tubetti
100 ml extra virgin olive oil
2 cloves garlic, thinly sliced
fresh or dried chilli, to taste
roughly chopped flat-leaf parsley, to garnish

Place the potato in a large heavy-based saucepan with 4 litres water and bring to the boil. Add a flat tablespoon of salt (more if needed), then add the pasta and cook for 10 minutes or until al dente.

Meanwhile, heat the olive oil in a large frying pan over low heat, add the garlic and as much chilli as you like and cook gently – you don't want to burn the garlic. Drain the pasta and potato, reserving a cup of the cooking water, and add to the garlic and chilli oil. Increase the heat to medium and toss everything together for 2 minutes, adding as much or as little pasta water as required. Scatter some parsley over the top and serve hot.

PASTA AND POTATO CRACKLE

PASTA e PATATE SFRITTA

by Michele Federico

PASTA AND CHICKPEA STEW

PASTA E CECI

by Rosetta D'Urso

Rosetta is the queen of the chickpea stew, just as Adolfo is the king of the bean stew (see page 132). I think her secret is the large quantity of fresh parsley she adds halfway through the cooking time. Although Rosetta does not offer freshly grated parmesan with the finished dish, I like to give people the option when I make it at home.

SERVES 6

600 g dried chickpeas
large pinch of bicarbonate of soda
4–5 cloves garlic, peeled and left whole
1 rosemary sprig, plus extra sprigs to garnish
1 cherry tomato (yes just one!)
½ hot chilli, chopped (optional)
1 large bunch flat-leaf parsley, leaves picked
1 tablespoon salt, plus more if needed
450 g mixed broken pasta (take all the odd bits of pasta
    left in the pantry and break them up into similar-sized pieces)
white pepper
200 ml extra virgin olive oil, or to taste

Soak the chickpeas in plenty of water overnight, with a pinch of bicarbonate of soda. Drain.

You can make the stew in a pressure cooker or in a heavy-based flameproof casserole dish on the stovetop.

If making it in a pressure cooker, put the chickpeas, garlic, rosemary, tomato and chilli (if using) in the pot and pour in enough water to come 6 cm above the level of the chickpeas. Cook for 1 hour, then release the steam manually. When it is safe, open the pressure cooker and add the parsley and salt, then cover and cook with slightly less pressure for another 30 minutes. Leave to cool in the pot.

If cooking on the stovetop, put the chickpeas, garlic, rosemary, tomato and chilli (if using) in the casserole dish and pour in enough water to come 6 cm above the chickpeas. Cover and bring to the boil, then reduce the heat and cook over low heat for 2 hours, checking the water level often and replenishing as required. Add the parsley and salt, then cover and cook for another hour.

You can make the stew to this point a day ahead, if liked.

Check the pot or casserole dish and make sure the liquid level is at least 2 cm above the level of the chickpeas. Top up with extra water if needed. Bring to the boil (without the lid if using a pressure cooker) and add the pasta. Taste and add more salt if needed, then simmer for 10–15 minutes or until the pasta is just cooked through. Taste again – the pasta takes away a lot of the salt flavour so you may need to add some more. Stir in some white pepper and plenty of oil, garnish with extra rosemary then enjoy with a good appetite.

NOTES *You'll need to soak the chickpeas overnight so start this a day or two before you want to eat it.*

Make sure you don't overdo the rosemary or it will completely overwhelm the chickpea flavour.

ADDING BROKEN PASTA PIECES TO A STEW WILL GIVE A SUPER-CREAMY RESULT, AS LONG AS THERE IS ENOUGH WATER (YOU CAN ALWAYS ADD BOILING WATER IF IT STARTS TO DRY OUT BEFORE THE PASTA IS READY). THE PASTA ABSORBS THE LIQUID AS IT COOKS, RELEASING ITS STARCHES TO MAKE A LOVELY CREAMY BASE.

ALWAYS ADD BICARBONATE OF SODA TO THE WATER WHEN SOAKING DRIED PULSES – THIS WILL HELP THEM OPEN BETTER FOR THE FOLLOWING DAY'S COOKING PROCESS. YOU CAN ALSO ADD THE JUICE OF HALF A LEMON TO HELP THE PULSES FERMENT BEFORE COOKING. THIS WAY THEY PRODUCE LESS GAS! YIKES!

ANCIENT DUMPLINGS IN TRADITIONAL NUT AND ANCHOVY SAUCE

N'DUNDERI TRADIZIONALI

by Massimo Proto

N'dunderi is the most ancient pasta in the Campania region, and dates back hundreds of years. It originated in the town of Minori, where Massimo was born. I have eaten various interpretations of these giant dumplings but none of them compare to Massimo's, which are light and exquisite. Here is his recipe in its most traditional form, served with anchovies and nuts.

SERVES 6
4 tablespoons extra virgin olive oil
1 clove garlic, peeled and left whole
8 anchovies under oil or salt, rinsed well
8 whole walnuts, roughly chopped
8 small hazelnuts, roughly chopped
30 g parmesan, grated
dill sprigs, to garnish

DUMPLINGS
1 kg fresh ricotta
400 g strong plain flour (such as Italian '00')
3 egg yolks
100 g parmesan, grated

To make the dumplings, place the flour on a clean surface and make a large well in the middle. Pass the ricotta through a ricer, then place it in the well, along with the egg yolks and parmesan. Mix all the ingredients together, working lightly and quickly with your hands – take care not to overwork this light dough, otherwise you will require more flour which will make the dumplings hard.

On a floured surface, roll the dough into 5 cm thick ropes, then cut into 3 cm lengths. Press lightly onto a floured fork to make creases to trap the sauce.

Bring a large saucepan of salted water to the boil. Gently drop in the dumplings a handful at a time (so the water doesn't lose too much heat) and scoop them out with a slotted spoon as soon as they rise to the surface. This should take 4–5 minutes.

Meanwhile, heat the oil in a large frying pan over low heat, add the garlic clove and cook until golden. Remove the garlic. Add the anchovies and cook gently until they melt into the oil, then add the nuts and cook for 10 seconds only, adding 3–4 tablespoons of the dumpling cooking water.

Transfer the dumplings straight from the saucepan to the sauce and toss lightly to coat. Add the parmesan just before serving, then garnish with dill sprigs and eat immediately.

THIS ANCIENT DISH IS THE ANCESTOR OF THE FAMOUS GNOCCHI. IT WAS DEVELOPED IN THE NEIGHBOURING TOWN OF MINORI, JUST A CURVE AWAY FROM THE TORRE NORMANNA, AND DATES BACK HUNDREDS OF YEARS.

IT IS MIND-BLOWING TO THINK THAT IT IS NOW BEING SERVED BY MASSIMO IN THE TORRE NORMANNA, WHICH WAS CONSTRUCTED BETWEEN 1250 AND 1300, MOST LIKELY AROUND THE TIME THE N'DUNDERI DUMPLING FIRST SAW THE LIGHT OF DAY!

Carla has been cooking this recipe for decades and has really made it her own. She purees the sauce, which becomes opaque and creamy-looking, but without a hint of cream – just parmesan to highlight its flavours. Coupled with baby macaroni, this baked treat is heavenly but very rich. You'll only need a small serving.

SERVES 6-8

100 ml extra virgin olive oil
1½ large white onions, roughly chopped
2 medium carrots, roughly chopped
1 large stick celery, roughly chopped
150 g minced beef with a bit of fat
125 ml white wine
salt
50 g butter
4 tablespoons strong plain flour (such as Italian '00')
500 g short pasta (preferably baby penne)
200 g parmesan, grated
240 g prosciutto, cut into 3 mm wide strips
240 g fontina or emmental cheese, cut into 3 mm wide strips

Heat the oil in a large, deep frying pan over medium heat, add the onion, carrot, celery and beef and cook until golden and slightly sticking to the base. Pour in the white wine and boil until it has evaporated, then add 1 litre hot water and a large pinch of salt. Bring to the boil, then reduce the heat and simmer over low heat for 1 hour. Transfer to a blender and blend until smooth (or use a stick blender).

Melt the butter in a large frying pan, add the flour and stir until combined. Add the beef and vegetable puree and bring to the boil over medium–high heat. Taste and season with salt if needed, then set aside to cool completely.

Preheat the oven to 180°C (fan-forced).

Cook the pasta in boiling salted water for 8–10 minutes or until al dente. Drain and mix with half the beef and vegetable sauce. Stir in 150 g parmesan.

Spoon the pasta mixture into small ovenproof dishes and cover with the remaining sauce. Scatter over strips of prosciutto and fontina or emmental then sprinkle with the remaining parmesan. Bake for 5–10 minutes or until warmed through and the cheese has melted. If you have made these ahead of time and stored them in the fridge, increase the cooking time to 15 minutes.

BAKED PASTA ALLA GENOVESE

PASTA AL FORNO ALLA GENOVESE

by Carla Rispoli

ACCORDING TO LEGEND, THERE WAS ONCE A NEAPOLITAN COOK CALLED GENOVESE WHO WAS SO PROUD OF A SCRUMPTIOUS PASTA DISH HE'D CREATED THAT HE NAMED IT PASTA GENOVESE! IT HAS SINCE BECOME AN ICONIC DISH ALL OVER CAMPANIA.

HOMEMADE RAVIOLI FILLED WITH BUFFALO RICOTTA AND CHERRY TOMATO SAUCE

RAVIOLI IMBOTTITI CON RICOTTA DI BUFALA E SALSA DI POMODORINI

by Fortunata Cilento

These ravioli just melt in your mouth – pillows of creamy ricotta on a cloud of sweet tomatoes. Absolute bliss. Ricotta made from buffalo milk is available in some larger supermarkets, but if you can't find it, regular cow's milk ricotta is fine. Just make sure it's fresh.

SERVES 6
grated parmesan, to serve
basil leaves, to garnish

RAVIOLI DOUGH
salt
300 g strong plain flour (such as Italian '00')
1 egg and 1 egg yolk, lightly beaten together

RICOTTA FILLING
300 g fresh ricotta (preferably buffalo ricotta)
100 g mascarpone
50 g buffalo mozzarella, cut into small dice
50 g parmesan, grated
1 teaspoon finely chopped marjoram
    (or a pinch of dried marjoram)
pinch of salt

CHERRY TOMATO SAUCE
2½ tablespoons extra virgin olive oil
1 clove garlic, peeled and squashed
1 kg sweet cherry tomatoes, cut in half

To make the ravioli dough, pour 300 ml water into a medium saucepan, add a pinch of salt and bring to the boil. Add the flour, then remove from the heat and stir constantly for 5 minutes or until amalgamated. Pour onto a lightly floured work surface (marble is best) and knead lightly and quickly for 10 minutes. Transfer the dough to a glass bowl and add the beaten egg, then knead on the work surface until well incorporated. Return to the bowl, cover with plastic film and rest in the fridge for at least 30 minutes.

To make the ricotta filling, combine all the ingredients in a bowl.

Place the dough on a large well-floured surface and roll out as thinly as possible with a floured rolling pin (it should be 2–3 mm thick). Brush half the dough lightly with cold water, then dollop heaped teaspoons of filling onto the dough, leaving a 1–1.5 cm space between each one. You don't want too much pasta around the filling. Fold over the other side of the dough to cover the filling like a blanket.

Using a 5 cm glass or biscuit cutter, cut out each ravioli with the filling in the centre. A blunt-edged glass is the best as it cuts the soft dough and seals each ravioli at the same time; if the ravioli are not sealed, gently press them closed with a fork or with your fingers.

For the sauce, heat the oil in a medium frying pan over medium–low heat, add the garlic clove and cook until golden. Remove the garlic. Increase the heat to high, add the cherry tomatoes and toss for 5 minutes. For an extra creamy sauce, let the tomatoes cool a little then pass them through a fine-mesh sieve to remove the skins.

Bring 3 litres water to the boil in a large saucepan and add plenty of salt. Carefully drop in the ravioli, a few at a time, and cook for 5 minutes or until they rise to the surface. Remove with a slotted spoon and add to the tomato sauce. Warm quickly over high heat then spoon into pasta bowls. Serve with grated parmesan and a couple of basil leaves for perfume.

HOMEMADE PASTA WITH ARTICHOKES

SCIALATIELLI CON I CARCIOFI

by Fortunata Cilento

Scialatielli is a well-known homemade pasta thought by many to have derived from this area; however, historian Ezio Falcone believes it was originally brought to the Amalfi Coast from La Calabria region of southern Italy by the famous 1960s chef of La Caravella restaurant in Amalfi (strangely, no one can remember his name!). Whichever way, these days there are few restaurants along this coastline that do not offer at least one version. This is one of my favourites as Fortunata is a genius when it comes to making pasta.

SERVES 6

3 large artichokes (purple ones if you can find them)
2½ tablespoons extra virgin olive oil
1 clove garlic, peeled and left whole
200 ml vegetable stock
salt and pepper
50 g parmesan, grated, plus extra to serve (optional)
roughly chopped flat-leaf parsley, to garnish

SCIALATIELLI DOUGH

500 g strong plain flour (such as Italian '00')
100 g durum wheat flour
300 ml milk
1 egg

To make the scialatielli dough, place all the ingredients in a bowl and mix together well. Turn out onto a floured surface and knead energetically until smooth and elastic. Place in a bowl and cover with plastic film, then rest in the fridge for 10–15 minutes. Roll out the dough on a floured surface to a thickness of about 3 mm – ideally it should be a rectangle about 12–13 cm wide. Roll up the dough widthways or lengthways, depending on how long you want the strips to be, and cut into 1 cm-wide strips. You may need to dust the dough with extra flour to stop it sticking.

To clean the artichokes, break off all the tough outer leaves until you reach the very pale leaves, and trim off any spikes from the top with some scissors. Chop off the stems and shave off the dark exterior. Cut the artichokes in half and scoop out the slightly hairy middle (if present), then cut these halves in half again and slice very thinly.

Heat the oil in a large frying pan over medium–low heat, add the garlic clove and cook until golden. Remove the garlic. Add the artichoke and cook for 5 minutes or until al dente. Add 2–3 tablespoons hot water and cook for another 5–8 minutes or until the water has evaporated, then pour in the stock and simmer until slightly reduced. Season to taste with salt and pepper.

Meanwhile, cook the scialatielli in boiling salted water for 6–8 minutes or until tender but still al dente. Drain and add to the artichokes, then toss over high heat until the sauce is a good consistency but the pasta is not overcooked. Stir in the parmesan just before serving to bulk up the sauce. Sprinkle with chopped parsley and serve immediately with extra parmesan, if liked.

NOTE *I am a big lover of 'la pasta asciutta' (dried pasta from the pack which comes in a zillion varieties and qualities) as it can be eaten very al dente. This is harder to achieve with homemade pastas like scialatielli, which are softer. But if they are dressed well and have just the right amount of durum wheat and 00 flour, I become a total convert!*

FORTUNATA (LEFT) WITH SISTER FILOMENA

Fortunata CILENTO

POSITANO, RESTAURANT OWNER AND CHEF

Not far from the ancient ruins of Pompeii lies a small village called Vico Equense, which is famous for its pizza al metro (pizza by the metre). I must have devoured at least a few kilometres of this tasty dish over the years. This is Fortunata's home town, but as a young school teacher she met a nice boy from Positano and her destiny changed drastically. She came to live on the Amalfi Coast, where they started a taverna/B&B, and the rest is history.

Luckily for her husband Antonio, Fortunata had a history (and talent) with food. I've been eating in her taverna for nearly three decades now and have watched her children grow, her business flourish and her cooking talents excel. She's also the humblest of humble cooks.

Filled with family and talented young assistant chefs, her kitchen is very busy. Fortunata is a great believer in organic produce and wholesome cooking. In fact, when we last met she was running off to the nearby town of Gragnano, where they make some of the best pasta in southern Italy, to buy a 150-year-old lievito madre (a mother acid or natural yeast) to make her own sourdough breads. The taverna has always served excellent breads.

Everything runs like clockwork in Fortunata's kitchen. Her food history started as a child when she fell under the spell of an aunt who was a capable pastry chef. Fortunata absorbed all she could and her dreams of working with food eventually became a reality. She not only makes a great sponge, she is a sponge for any new knowledge about food. 'It's all about precision, science and mathematics,' she says about pastry cooking.

She's studied religiously for years under the watchful eye of Laura Niccolai, a renowned Sorrentine cook, now well over eighty years old, who not only has a prestigious cooking school in Italy, but has also found success over the years in New York. Unlike many other proficient chefs, Fortunata continues to seek instruction. She feels you can never stop learning when it comes to culinary skills, and one of her dreams is to travel to India and Japan to learn their cooking techniques and traditions. Owning a super-busy, constantly full restaurant and running a well-staffed kitchen, it's little wonder Fortunata's secret ambition is to find time for her true passion: cooking alone.

FORTUNATA'S RECIPES

Margherita delGIUDICE

MAIORI, MOTHER OF TWO AND TRAFFIC WARDEN

Margherita is from the town of Maiori in the heart of the Amalfi coastline. I love this women and her flair for flavours – when she was just twenty she would guess the exact ingredients in restaurant dishes, then go away and invent her own dish using the same ingredients! She is a complete natural in the kitchen and is known for it all over town, although her two kids are her harshest critics when it comes to home cooking.

Like so many of her generation, she headed north many years ago to find work in a restaurant. When the chef was away sick Margherita would take over, and she quickly became the locals' favourite. She opened her own restaurant for a short time before her husband was transferred back to their native Maiori where today she cooks for her family and is a part-time traffic cop!

MARGHERITA'S RECIPES

Michele FEDERICO

BORN IN POMPEII, LIVES IN MILANO, PLAYS IN POSITANO

Michele resides in Milano, where he works with antiques, and relaxes in Positano. He is driven by a heart and soul filled with the aromas and flavours of Neapolitan recipes. Michele's cooking philosophy is simple: if you add a large pinch of passion, a good chunk of your heart and a generous cup of goodwill, everything you prepare will be pleasantly appetising for your guests. He swears it works every time.

Michele has buckets of talent in the kitchen, and has dedicated a good part of his life to giving friends and family immense pleasure at the dinner table. He is well aware of the traditional secrets of the Amalfi Coast and its natural produce, but he will often add a hint of something from Pompeii or the north of Italy. He loves nothing better than to walk the mountainous regions of the Amalfi Coast above Positano and Praiano, searching for his favourite aromatics for his melting pot!

MICHELE'S RECIPES

LINGUINE WITH VONGOLE

On the Amalfi Coast this dish is as popular as the meat pie is in Australia! And like the pie, there are plenty of versions. It can be eaten with a tomato base or a clear one; some use wine, while others depend only on the clams' natural juices; some swear by that hint of chilli, while others claim it destroys the flavour. Whichever way you like it, as long as it's prepared with love and fresh produce, this dish is a winner. Vera's recipe is simple and perfect, and a great way to get your appetite fired up for the rest of the meal.

LINGUINE WITH VONGOLE

LINGUINE CON LE VONGOLE

by Vera Milano

SERVES 6

400 g linguine
150 ml extra virgin olive oil, plus extra to serve
1 clove garlic, finely chopped
fresh or dried chilli, to taste (optional)
24 cherry tomatoes, cut in half
500 g clams, well purged of sand
handful of flat-leaf parsley, roughly chopped

Cook the linguine in boiling salted water for 8 minutes or until al dente. Drain the pasta, reserving a cup of the cooking water in case you need it for the sauce.

Meanwhile, heat the oil in a large heavy-based frying pan over medium-low heat, add the garlic and chilli (if using) and cook until golden. Add the tomatoes and clams, then cover the pan and cook for about 5 minutes until the clams open. Discard any that do not open.

Add the pasta to the clams, which should have given a decent amount of juice during their very brief cooking time, and toss together for just a minute or two. Add a small amount of pasta water if necessary. Remove from the heat and toss through the parsley. Drizzle with a little extra oil and serve immediately.

ALWAYS PURGE YOUR CLAMS FOR AN HOUR OR TWO BEFORE COOKING THEM IN SALTED WATER. QUICKLY TAP THEM TOGETHER WHILE RINSING UNDER COLD WATER — IF ANY SOUND SOLID, DITCH'EM! THEY COULD BE FULL OF SAND, AND ONE SANDY CLAM COULD RUIN THE ENTIRE DISH!

Margherita's kids give this recipe their No 1 vote; in fact, this is a kids' favourite up and down the Amalfi Coast. So simple to make, and you can add extra ingredients to suit your tastes. I love to add some chives for that little extra kick and ripped basil leaves at the end before serving.

BAKED SPAGHETTI SALAD

SPAGHETTI AL FORNO

by Margherita del Giudice

SERVES 6

500 g truss or oxheart tomatoes, cut into cubes
2 × 185 g cans tuna, drained and flaked
10 salted capers, rinsed and drained
300 g Sicilian olives
4 tablespoons extra virgin olive oil
1 teaspoon fresh or dried oregano
3 tablespoons fresh breadcrumbs made from stale bread (see page 30)
salt
500 g spaghetti

Preheat the oven to 200°C (fan-forced).

Place the tomato, tuna, capers, olives, olive oil, oregano, 1 tablespoon breadcrumbs and salt to taste in a large bowl. Gently toss to combine.

Meanwhile, cook the spaghetti in boiling salted water until very al dente (about half the cooking time specified on the packet). Drain and rinse under cold water, then drain again and add to the salad.

Line a well-oiled baking dish with 1 tablespoon breadcrumbs, add the pasta salad and scatter the remaining breadcrumbs over the top. Bake in the oven for 10–15 minutes. Yum! The kids will love it.

HEARTY BEAN AND PASTA STEW

PASTA E FAGIOLI

by Daniele Bella

This is real comfort food, as most humble dishes are, yet today it is enjoyed by noblemen and fishermen alike all over Italy. Adolfo spent a good part of the war years living off what grew on the side of the road and became an expert at cooking this type of food. He shared all his hints with Daniele, and eventually many were passed on to me. With this recipe, the most important thing is that the beans must be well cooked, not al dente.

SERVES 4

200 g dried cannellini beans
salt
pinch of bicarbonate of soda
2 cloves garlic, finely chopped
250 g diced vegetables (such as celery, carrot and potato)
50 g piece of pancetta
50 g piece of parmesan crust
½ small hot chilli, chopped (optional)
200 g mixed broken pasta (whatever you have in the cupboard)
½ white onion, finely chopped
3 tablespoons extra virgin olive oil

Soak the cannellini beans in plenty of water overnight, with a pinch of salt and bicarbonate of soda. Drain.

Place the beans in a large heavy-based stewing pot (the heavier the better – iron or ceramic are good) and add the garlic, vegetables, pancetta, parmesan crust and chilli (if using). Pour in enough water to cover the ingredients by 5–6 cm, then cover with a lid and bring to the boil. Reduce the heat and cook, covered, for 2–2½ hours or until the beans are well cooked. You can do this part of the recipe in advance, if liked.

When you are ready to eat, bring the mixture to the boil and add the pasta and a good pinch of salt. Stir well and make sure there is enough liquid to cover the ingredients by 3–4 cm, then cook over high heat, stirring occasionally, until the pasta is nice and tender (not al dente). Most of the liquid should have been absorbed into the pasta and beans by this point, but add hot water if the mixture has dried up during cooking; conversely, if the pasta is nearly ready and you have too much liquid, scoop out the excess with a ladle and boil the remainder until thickened. Taste and check for salt.

Spoon the stew into bowls and top with a teaspoon of raw onion and a dessertspoon of oil.

NOTE *If you have one, this recipe is best made in a pressure cooker. Add the ingredients to the pot, as described in the recipe, then cover with 7–8 cm water and cook for 1¼–1½ hours. Leave to cool, then release the steam and remove the lid. Bring to the boil again, then add the pasta and salt and check the water level. Cook and serve as above.*

Potato bake has long been a favourite all over the world, with cooks in every country adding their own personal touches, but there is something about the Bella family recipe that shines a light above the others. It is definitely a meal in itself and is well loved by locals and visitors up and down the Amalfi Coast.

SERVES 8

150 g fresh breadcrumbs made from stale bread (see page 30)
1 kg pontiac potatoes
60 g butter
2 eggs, lightly beaten
200 ml milk
250 g mozzarella, cut into 1 cm dice
70 g parmesan, grated
2 eggs, extra, boiled, peeled and cut into quarters
250 g Italian salami, cut into 1 cm dice
sea salt
basil leaves, to garnish (optional)

Preheat the oven to 180°C (fan-forced). Grease a 35 cm × 25 cm baking dish and sprinkle with some of the breadcrumbs.

Boil the potatoes in their skins until tender. Drain and leave to cool slightly, then peel and press through a ricer or mash with a potato masher.

Place the mashed potato in a large bowl and stir in the butter, then gently mix in the beaten egg, milk, mozzarella, parmesan, boiled egg and salami. Season well with salt, then dollop into the baking dish. Sprinkle the remaining breadcrumbs evenly over the top and bake for 30 minutes or until golden on top and the mozzarella has melted. Garnish with basil leaves, if liked.

TRADITIONAL POTATO BAKE

GATEAU DI PATATE

by Daniele Bella

BECAUSE OF ITS HUMBLE YET HEARTY INGREDIENTS, WE CAN ONLY ASSUME POTATO BAKE WAS ORIGINALLY A SIMPLE 'POOR MAN'S' DISH SERVED UP DURING THE COLDER MONTHS OF THE YEAR WHEN THE LOCAL POTATOES WERE AT THEIR BEST.

CREAMY SCAMPI RISOTTO

RISOTTO ALLA CREMA DI SCAMPI

by Roberto Proto

I actually feel quite smug about having this recipe. It is an all-time favourite up and down the Amalfi Coast and the recipe is well guarded at Roberto and Massimo's little trattoria in Atrani. EVERYONE in the area has tried it, but few have worked out the secret of its success! Until now . . .

SERVES 6

480 g carnaroli rice
1 kg cleaned scampi
250 ml extra virgin olive oil
150 ml Cognac
750 ml thickened cream
1½ tablespoons tomato ketchup
2 teaspoons Tabasco sauce
salt and pepper
flat-leaf parsley sprigs, to garnish

Bring 750 ml lightly salted water to the boil, add the rice and simmer for 10 minutes. Drain and rinse well. It's important to rid the rice of all the starch (unlike a traditional risotto where the starch is a vital component). You can cook the rice the day before and store it in the fridge, if liked.

Peel the scampi (reserving the heads for later) and chop them into medium-sized pieces.

Heat the oil in a large heavy-based frying pan over medium heat, add the chopped scampi and cook for 5 minutes or until it has changed colour and absorbed its liquid. Pour in the Cognac. Shake the pan to get a nice big flame and cook until it has evaporated. Add the cream, ketchup and Tabasco, then remove the pan from the heat and give it a good stir.

Return the pan to medium heat and stir in 125 ml water. When the mixture comes to the boil, add the rice and cook for 10 minutes, stirring constantly. Season to taste. If the mixture is too thick, add a little more water.

Spoon the risotto into one large serving bowl or individual bowls and top with the scampi heads and parsley sprigs.

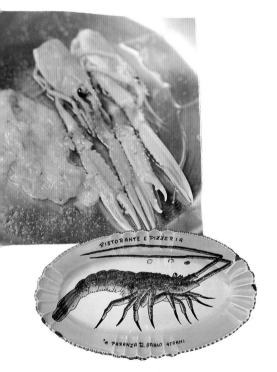

AFTER WORLD WAR II WHEN THE AMERICANS OCCUPIED THIS PART OF ITALY, A PASSIONATE AMERICAN COOK IN THE AREA WAS EXPERIMENTING WITH LOCAL INGREDIENTS AND SOME PRODUCTS FROM HOME. THIS CRAZY MIX HAS THE STARS AND STRIPES ALL OVER IT, BUT MIRACULOUSLY OUR ANONYMOUS CHEF HELD ONTO THE LOCAL FLAVOURS.

While researching this book, I often found myself eating this pasta dish at Fortunata's. It was so bloody good I kept going back for more. But what could I suggest as a substitute for the tiny calamari I'd only seen in Italy? Like the wonderful fresh anchovies, I was beginning to think that the baby calamari was another hidden treasure, but I was wandering through the Sydney fish markets recently and there they were in all their glory. A bit fiddly to clean but worth every mouthful. Start the tagliolini a day or two ahead if you can as it benefits from resting and drying out slightly.

SERVES 6

150 ml extra virgin olive oil
2 cloves garlic, peeled and squashed
200 g cherry tomatoes, cut in half
50 g pitted ligurian olives
400 g baby calamari, cleaned and cut into rings
2½ tablespoons brandy
roughly chopped flat-leaf parsley or basil, to garnish

TAGLIOLINI DOUGH

200 g strong plain flour (such as Italian '00')
100 g durum wheat flour
pinch of salt
2½ tablespoons extra virgin olive oil
1 egg
8–9 egg yolks

To make the tagliolini dough, place the flours and salt on a clean surface and mix together well. Make a well in the middle and add the oil. Drop in the whole egg and then eight egg yolks. Whether you need the ninth yolk depends on the size of the eggs, the humidity of the flour and how much white gets into the yolk when separating the eggs. With your fingers inside the well, slowly work your way outward until all the ingredients are amalgamated, then knead for 10 minutes. Place the dough in a bowl, cover with plastic film and rest in the fridge for at least 30 minutes, but no more than 3 hours. Alternatively leave the dough to dry uncovered overnight. This allows the pasta to lose its elasticity, making it easier to roll out.

Using a floured rolling pin, roll out the dough on a well-floured surface as thinly as possible (it should be about 1 mm thick). Cut into sheets that are about 20 cm wide (it doesn't matter how long they are) then roll up each sheet and cut 5 mm wide discs (very thin and delicious). Unravel your rolls loosely and let the pasta strips dry out on a wooden surface or large linen table cloth. For best results, leave it this way overnight if you have time, as the pasta holds better during cooking when it is dried.

Heat half the oil in a large frying pan over medium–low heat, add one garlic clove and cook until golden. Remove the garlic. Increase the heat to high, add the tomatoes and cook for 5–10 minutes until you have a creamy orange sauce. The heat must be high but add the tomatoes immediately so the oil does not burn. Add the olives when the sauce is almost ready.

Heat the remaining oil in a separate frying pan over medium–low heat, add the remaining garlic clove and cook until golden. Remove the garlic. Increase the heat to high, then add the calamari and cook for just 3 minutes. Pour in the brandy and cook for 1–2 minutes until it has evaporated, then add the tomato sauce. Toss for 1 minute, then take the pan off the heat.

Meanwhile, cook the tagliolini in boiling salted water until they come to the surface. This will take about 3 minutes if the pasta has dried out overnight, less if made the same day. Drain, reserving a cup of the cooking water, and add to the calamari mixture. Toss over high heat for a few seconds, adding some of the reserved pasta water if the sauce is too thick. Garnish with parsley or basil and serve immediately.

HOMEMADE TAGLIOLINI WITH BLACK OLIVES AND BABY CALAMARI SAUCE

TAGLIOLINI CON OLIVE NERE E CALAMARETTI

by Fortunata Cilento

IF YOU ARE LUCKY ENOUGH TO FIND THE TINY CALAMARI AT THE FISH MARKETS, COOK THEM WHOLE, THEN REMOVE THE HEAD AND CARTILAGE FROM INSIDE BUT RESERVE THE TENTACLES. RINSE THEM UNDER COLD WATER AS YOU GO, THEN PAT DRY. IT'S A LITTLE EXTRA WORK FOR A BIG BONUS IN FLAVOUR!

CALAMARI OR SQUID RISOTTO

RISOTTO DI CALAMARI O TOTANI

by Daniele Bella

This risotto dish is so flavoursome with just the calamari as a base, it doesn't even require a broth – plain old boiling water will do the trick. Squid will give a stronger sea flavour, while calamari is more delicate. Either way, it is a champion dish that will have your dinner guests begging for more, so make plenty!

SERVES 4

3 tablespoons extra virgin olive oil
1 clove garlic, finely chopped
4 calamari or squid tubes, cleaned and cut into 1 cm squares
salt
100 g cherry tomatoes, cut in half
350 g carnaroli rice
3 tablespoons roughly chopped flat-leaf parsley
lemon wedges, to serve (optional)

Heat the oil in a large heavy-based saucepan over medium heat, add the garlic and cook until golden. Add the calamari or squid and salt to taste and cook, covered, for 45 minutes, stirring occasionally. This little mollusc will generate its own liquid after a very short time but check every 10 minutes to make sure it doesn't dry out. Top up with water, if necessary. Add the tomato halves for the last 5 minutes of cooking.

Have 2 litres boiling water ready. Increase the heat under the calamari or squid to medium–high, add the rice and toss until well coated. Add a ladle of boiling water and cook, stirring constantly, until the water has been completely absorbed. Add the remaining water in this way – it should take 18–20 minutes, depending how al dente you like your risotto. Stir through the parsley just before serving and serve with lemon wedges, if liked.

THERE IS AN EXPRESSION IN ITALIAN THAT REFERS TO THE COOKING TIME OF MOLLUSCS: 'SNAPPY OR SLOW – ANYTHING IN BETWEEN WILL MAKE THEM AS TOUGH AS NAILS!' MANY COASTAL CHEFS BELIEVE MOLLUSCS SHOULD BE COOKED VERY QUICKLY TO LOCK IN THE SEA FLAVOURS, BUT THIS RECIPE OF DANIELE'S DISPROVES THIS THEORY!

SECONDI

FILLETED FISH ON LEMON LEAVES

FILETTO DI PESCE SULLE FOGLIE DI LIMONE

by Mario Rispoli

The two most commonly used ingredients on the Amalfi Coast today must be fish and lemon leaves, so it was only a matter of time before they were coupled together. The perfumed leaves of the famous Amalfi Sfusato lemon make an excellent baking dish – whatever cooks on top of them takes on a sparkling citrus flavour. I can't think of a more heavenly dish than the one Mario has developed here.

SERVES 6

250 ml fish stock, more if needed (see page 78 if you want to make your own)
100 ml extra virgin olive oil
salt and pepper
50 g fresh breadcrumbs made from stale bread (see page 30)
30 g parmesan, grated
6 × 150–200 g white fish fillets (snapper is perfect), skin and bones removed
about 20 large lemon leaves (more if the leaves are smaller)
lemon slices or wedges, to serve

Preheat the oven to 180°C (fan-forced).

Combine the stock, oil, salt and pepper in a shallow bowl. Pour the breadcrumbs and parmesan into a separate bowl and toss together.

Dip the fish fillets into the dressing, then coat with the breadcrumbs, shaking off any excess. Arrange the leaves, shiny-side down, in a baking dish and place the fish fillets on top. Bake for 10–15 minutes or until golden and cooked through. Serve with lemon and, if liked, a fresh green salad and a chilled glass of Fiano or Falanghina white wine.

MY FATHER-IN-LAW ADOLFO WAS ONE OF THE VERY FIRST TO DEVELOP 'LEMON-LEAF GRILLING'. HIS SPECIALTY WAS MOZZARELLA ON THE LEMON LEAF, WHICH YOU FIND IN MANY RESTAURANTS ON THE COAST TODAY, BUT NONE DO IT AS WELL AS DA ADOLFO RESTAURANT IN POSITANO. EVERY MORNING WE WOULD BE SENT INTO THE PRICKLY BUSHES OF WILD LEMON TREES BEHIND THE BEACH RESTAURANT TO COLLECT AS MANY BIG LEAVES AS POSSIBLE FOR THIS AMAZINGLY SIMPLE BUT DELICIOUS DISH.

KING CONRADIN MEATBALLS

POLPETTE ALLA CORRADINA

by Fortunata Cilento

Named after King Conradin of Sicily, this dish has a gruesome origin. While attempting to rightfully claim his throne, the teenage king was captured in battle by the ambitious Charles of Anjou (Charles I) and unceremoniously beheaded in Piazza del Mercato, Naples in 1268. Although this shocked the entire medieval world, Charles quickly established his possession of the crown of Sicily and Naples, and we were left with these scrumptious little meatballs in the memory of King Conradin. But don't dwell on the story too much – just enjoy them!

SERVES 6
2 eggs
50 g fresh breadcrumbs made from stale bread (see page 30)
50 g parmesan, grated, plus extra to serve
300 ml peanut oil
basil leaves, to garnish
crusty bread, to serve

MEATBALLS
300 g lean minced beef
300 g minced pork
100 g fresh breadcrumbs made from stale bread (see page 30)
100 g fresh ricotta
40 g parmesan, grated
2 eggs
salt and pepper

TOMATO SAUCE
100 ml extra virgin olive oil
1 clove garlic, peeled and left whole
1 kg cherry tomatoes, cut in half
salt
6 basil leaves, torn

To make the meatballs, place all the ingredients in a glass bowl and mix together with your hands. Form into meatballs about the size of golf balls.

Lightly whisk the eggs in a shallow bowl, and combine the breadcrumbs and parmesan in another bowl. Dip the meatballs in the egg and then in the breadcrumb mix until well coated.

Heat the peanut oil in a large heavy-based saucepan until hot but not smoking, add the meatballs (in batches if necessary) and cook until golden brown. Remove with a slotted spoon and drain on paper towels.

To make the tomato sauce, heat the oil in a large frying pan over medium–low heat, add the garlic clove and cook until golden. Remove the garlic. Increase the heat to high, add the tomatoes and cook for 5 minutes. Pass the sauce through a mouli or fine-meshed sieve, then return to the pan and season to taste with salt.

Add the meatballs to the tomato sauce and cook over low heat for 15–20 minutes. Stir through the torn basil at the very end. Serve with a sprinkling of parmesan and crusty bread, garnished with extra basil leaves.

NOTE *If you like, add 30 g raisins and 30 g pine nuts to the meatball mix. This is the old way.*

WHEN YOU COOK ANY TOMATO ON A NICE LIVELY FLAME FOR 10 MINUTES OR MORE, IT BECOMES A RICH ORANGE CREAMY CONSISTENCY, ESPECIALLY WHEN USING HALVED CHERRY TOMATOES. THIS IS A FUNDAMENTAL PART OF NEAPOLITAN COOKING.

On the Amalfi Coast walnuts are not just eaten as a nut, they are also considered one of the tastiest condiments available. Used in sauces, pasta toppings, cakes, biscuits, liqueur flavours and gelati, they also accompany mouth-watering cuts of meat. Here, Giuseppe has used flavoursome local produce to give the humble lamb cutlet a complete facelift.

SERVES 4

150 g fresh walnuts
500 g (about 12) lamb cutlets, not too thick
extra virgin olive oil, for cooking and drizzling
salt
1 clove garlic, squashed
½ hot chilli, finely chopped (optional)
200 g broccoli rabe or regular broccoli, well washed
6 sundried tomatoes, cut into thin strips

Finely chop the walnuts in a coffee grinder or similar until they reach the consistency of coarse breadcrumbs.

Brush the cutlets with oil and sprinkle salt on both sides, then coat with the chopped walnuts, like a rough hearty schnitzel.

Heat a barbecue grill plate to medium (use a heavy chargrill pan on the stove if you don't have a barbecue). Cook the cutlets for 2–3 minutes each side. Remove and rest for a few minutes.

Meanwhile, pour enough oil into a medium frying pan to just cover the base and heat over medium heat. Add the garlic clove and chilli (if using) and cook until golden. Remove the garlic. Add the broccoli and cook for 5 minutes or until al dente.

Divide the cutlets and broccoli among four plates and drizzle with a little oil. Decorate with strips of sundried tomato. Buon appetito!

NOTE *If you cannot find broccoli rabe (a slightly bitter leafy green) feel free to use regular broccoli, adding half a fresh chilli to make sure it holds its own next to these heavenly chops. Depending on how al dente you like your vegetables, you might want to blanch the regular broccoli for a few minutes before pan-frying it.*

GRILLED LAMB CUTLETS WITH WALNUTS ON BROCCOLI RABE

AGNELLO GRIGLIATO CON NOCI, SU CIME DI RAPE DI TRAMONTI

by Giuseppe Francese

PORK MEDALLIONS WITH RICH RED WINE SAUCE AND FRIED POTATO ROUNDS

FILETTO DI MAIALE AL TINTORE DI TRAMONTI CON PATATE A SCAGLIE

by Giuseppe Francese

I have a group of friends in the Positano area who are extremely adept during the autumn season of the maialata – pig-slaughtering season. They delight in recounting their efforts of coaxing and caressing the little beasts before doing them in to achieve the most tender, flavoursome meat. Even today, many locals, Giuseppe included, keep their own pigs. This dish is a champion example of this tradition.

SERVES 4

160 ml extra virgin olive oil
1 carrot, sliced
1 small onion, sliced
1 stick celery, sliced
500 ml rich red wine, plus extra if needed
1 teaspoon salt
1 teaspoon pepper
knob of butter
30 g plain flour
2 bay leaves
1 dessertspoon sugar
600 g pork medallions cut from pork fillet
4 thin slices pancetta
fried potato rounds (see page 192), to serve

Heat 2 tablespoons oil in a large heavy-based saucepan over medium heat, add the carrot, onion and celery and cook until the onion is golden. Add the wine, salt and pepper and boil for about 10 minutes or until the sauce has reduced. Blend the butter and flour together, then add to the pan, along with the bay leaves and sugar and stir until smooth. If the sauce is looking a little dry, add some more wine. Cook for a few minutes until reduced and thickened.

Wrap each pork medallion in a slice of pancetta. Heat 2 tablespoons oil in a heavy-based frying pan over high heat, add the medallions and cook until browned on both sides. Remove the pork, then drain the oil and wipe out the pan. Return the pork to the pan, pour the wine sauce over the top and cook over medium heat for 3 minutes.

Divide the pork medallions, sauce and vegetables among four plates. Finish each serve with a tablespoon of oil and serve with fried potato rounds. Also delicious with creamy mash.

PORK IS ONE OF THE TASTIEST MEATS ON THE AMALFI COAST. IT IS NOT SO COMMON IN RESTAURANTS ON THE COASTLINE, BUT FURTHER UP INTO THE MOUNTAINOUS REGIONS IT IS PLENTIFUL AND WIDELY FOUND IN LOCAL TRATTORIAS AND RESTAURANTS.

GIUSEPPE WITH WIFE ANTONELLA

Giuseppe FRANCESE

TRAMONTI, RESTAURANT OWNER AND CHEF

Giuseppe and his wife Antonella took off many years ago from their Amalfi Coast home town of Tramonti and headed to Varese in the north of Italy, to work in the restaurant of Giuseppe's brother. Year-round work can be limited in the south for the young and ambitious who want to improve their skills.

In Varese, Giuseppe learnt the art of refined cooking from a very capable and talented chef, and then, once he was feeling secure in his craft, opened a successful little eatery with Antonella. Ten years on, they both felt the tug of the Amalfi Coast and returned to the undulating hills of Tramonti like two homing pigeons. They immediately recognised a need in the area for a classy little eatery and opened Ristorante Antichi Sapori. Fast-forward seven years and Giuseppe has become well known not only for his fine cooking skills but also for his appearances on several national television cooking shows.

Like many upmarket Amalfi Coast restaurateurs, Giuseppe finds time during the quieter months of autumn and spring to offer cooking classes to coastal visitors. These excellent courses in his efficient restaurant kitchen are very hands-on, and naturally the clients get to devour everything they've prepared. He's a wonderful instructor, teaching the use of traditional flavours from the surrounding hills, but giving them a special, elegant touch with his unique presentation.

He now has his eye on an enchanting 'Relais' just down the road, which would allow him to fulfil his dream of offering magnificent lodgings together with fine dining. He plans to grow all the produce for his kitchen organically and to offer a holiday full of relaxation, magnificent food and glorious panoramas. I'm holding my breath.

Giuseppe's favourite dish to eat is the big fat spaghettone made by a local pasta producer since 1812, Vicidomini di Castel S. Giorgio, coupled with local Tramonti caciocavallo cheese (a type of hardened mozzarella), fresh basil and the famous Neapolitan San Marzano tomatoes. Giuseppe is as true as this dish and its similarly coloured partner, the Italian flag!

GIUSEPPE'S RECIPES

SALTED COD BAKED WITH POTATOES

BACCALÀ con LE PATATE

by Rosetta D'Urso

Baccalà is one of those things you either love or hate, and I believe it all comes down to the first-time experience. I was lucky enough to have a very good one. My father-in-law Adolfo used to prepare it for his daughter Melania, as it was one of her favourites. Like Rosetta, Adolfo would always soak his baccalà for at least three days, resulting in a wonderful flavoursome dish that was never over-salty.

SERVES 6

6 × 170 g pieces salted cod
100 ml extra virgin olive oil
1 clove garlic, finely chopped
1 white onion, finely chopped
½ small hot chilli, finely chopped
6 cherry tomatoes, cut into quarters
800 g pontiac potatoes, peeled and cut into wedges
2 tablespoons finely chopped flat-leaf parsley,
    plus extra sprigs to garnish
warm ciabatta, to serve

Soak the salted cod in water for 3–4 days, changing the water every day. Drain and set aside.

Heat the oil in a large heavy-based saucepan or flameproof casserole dish over medium heat, add the garlic, onion and chilli and cook until golden. Add the tomato and cook for 5 minutes, then add the soaked cod, potato and chopped parsley. Pour in enough water to cover the fish, then enough to cover by two-thirds again. Bring to the boil, then reduce the heat and simmer, covered, for 30 minutes.

Remove the lid and cook for another 10 minutes or until some of the liquid has evaporated and the potato is tender. Shake the pan occasionally but do not turn the fish pieces or potato.

Spoon into shallow bowls or into one large serving bowl, then garnish with parsley sprigs and serve with plenty of warm ciabatta.

BACCALÀ OR SALT-CURED CODFISH WAS FIRST SEEN AROUND THE END OF THE 1400s, WHEN THE COMMON COD WAS DISCOVERED IN ABUNDANCE IN CHILLY SCANDINAVIAN WATERS. THE CLEVER FISHERMEN OF THE TIME KNEW THEY WERE ONTO A GOOD FOOD SUPPLY FOR THEIR LONG VOYAGES. THEY SIMPLY GUTTED AND CLEANED THE COD, DOUSED IT IN PLENTY OF SALT IN LARGE WOODEN VATS AND VOILA! BACCALÀ WAS BORN. THIS WAY OF PRESERVING FOOD (ESPECIALLY FISH) WAS COMPLETELY IN TUNE WITH THE DISPENSARIES OF ANCIENT TIMES ON THE AMALFI COAST AND THIS IS NOT AN UNCOMMON DISH IN THIS AREA, MAINLY FOUND IN THE HOME RATHER THAN AT RESTAURANTS.

STUFFED SQUID

TOTANI IMBOTTITI

by Pasquale Marino

I loved to eat this delicious rich dish most of all during winter when I had a woodchopper's appetite. The wonderful cooking smells would draw me to the kitchen like a magnet on the days Adolfo had the inclination to cook it. Luckily, it was also one of his favourites, so it was a regular at our table. Pasquale offers an equally delicious recipe with added cheese.

SERVES 6

180 ml extra virgin olive oil
800 g squid, well cleaned, tentacles removed and cut into 1 cm pieces
100 g fresh breadcrumbs made from stale bread (see page 30)
100 g smoked provola cheese, cut into small dice
50 g parmesan, grated
2 tablespoons finely chopped flat-leaf parsley
pinch of fresh or dried oregano
4 eggs
2 teaspoons salt
1 white onion, finely chopped
150 ml white wine
750 g tomatoes, cut into 1 cm dice
500 g spaghetti or penne (optional)
basil or flat-leaf parsley leaves, to garnish (optional)

Heat 3 tablespoons oil in a heavy-based frying pan over medium heat and cook the chopped tentacles for 10 minutes or until they change colour.

Combine the tentacles, breadcrumbs, provola, parmesan, parsley, oregano, eggs and 1 teaspoon salt in a bowl, mixing well with your fingers to achieve a sticky paste.

Stuff the squid tubes with the paste, taking care not to overfill them as they will swell during cooking. Secure the openings with a toothpick or two.

Heat the remaining oil in a large heavy-based frying pan over medium heat, add the onion and cook until golden. Add the stuffed squid and cook for about 10 minutes, turning frequently to brown all sides. Add the wine, tomato and remaining salt, then reduce the heat to low and cook for a further 15–20 minutes, turning occasionally. Test the squid by piercing them with a fork – if it goes through easily, the squid are ready. If there is too much sauce left in the pan, increase the heat and boil until reduced, but remember you need quite a bit of sauce to dress your pasta.

Meanwhile, if serving with pasta, cook the pasta in boiling salted water until al dente. Drain, reserving a cup of the cooking water.

Remove the squid from sauce and cut into thick slices. Toss the pasta through the tomato sauce (if using), adding some of the pasta water if necessary, then divide among shallow bowls. Arrange the squid discs on top and garnish with basil or parsley, if liked. Serve immediately.

While compiling these recipes I acquired more recipes for fish soup than I knew existed, but Giuliano's drew me in for two reasons. Firstly, for its amazing ingredients list that literally uses EVERYTHING you can pull from the sea; and secondly, the fact that Giuliano is the son of a fisherman and knows more about loving, eating, talking to and cooking fish than anyone I have ever met! He suggests you get the freshest local seafood available for his majestic soup.

ICONIC AMALFI COAST FISH SOUP

ZUPPA DI PESCE

by Giuliano Donatantonio

SERVES 4

120 ml extra virgin olive oil
4 cloves garlic, chopped
100 g octopus (about 4 small ones), well cleaned
300 g cuttlefish (about 2), well cleaned and cut in half
200 g calamari tubes (about 2), well cleaned and cut into rings
250 ml white wine
500 g cherry tomatoes, cut in half
1 × 800 g–1 kg grouper fish, scaled and gutted
1 × 800 g–1 kg anglerfish, scaled and gutted
1 × 800 g–1 kg rock fish (such as scorpion or turbot), scaled and gutted
4 king prawns, peeled and deveined
4 scampi
500 g clams, well purged of sand
500 g mussels, scrubbed and debearded
flat-leaf parsley leaves, to garnish
1 hot chilli, finely chopped (optional)
8 slices ciabatta bread, grilled

Heat 2 tablespoons oil in a large deep heavy-based frying pan over medium–low heat, add half the garlic and cook until lightly golden (make sure it doesn't burn). Add the octopus, cuttlefish, calamari and 125 ml wine and cook until the wine has evaporated. Add the tomatoes and simmer for 40 minutes.

Heat the remaining oil in a very large heavy-based flameproof casserole dish over low heat, add the remaining garlic and cook gently until golden. Add the three whole fish, remaining wine and the mollusc mixture, then cover and simmer for 30 minutes.

Add the prawns, scampi, clams and mussels. As soon as the clams and mussels open, the soup is pronto! (Discard any that don't open.)

Sprinkle with parsley and chilli (if using) and serve with freshly grilled ciabatta toast.

NOTE *To fully appreciate this dish, it should be eaten at least 6–8 hours after your last 'light' meal so you are close to starvation point. Eat heartily and don't be embarrassed to wear a bib! This is a truly important dish and you will need little else to accompany it.*

RICH BAKED PASTA PIE

TIMBALLO

by Tanina Vanacore

This is another Neapolitan dish enjoyed over the years by the noble classes, with a rich meaty content that only the well-heeled could afford. Tanina's mother spent many decades working as a cook in the more privileged kitchens of Naples, and Tanina spent much of her childhood watching the elaborate preparations. You will find many variations of this dish all over Campania but Tanina's is a classic – straight from her mother. You'll need to start the recipe at least one day ahead.

SERVES 10

300 g rigatoni
salt and pepper
50 g parmesan, grated
1 egg, lightly beaten

SHORTCRUST PASTRY

500 g strong plain flour (such as Italian '00')
250 g butter, softened
120 ml cold water
salt and pepper

RAGU SAUCE

350 ml extra virgin olive oil
2 large white onions, roughly chopped
12 pork rib strips, cut from the belly, fat removed
  (ask your butcher to do this)
400 g Italian pork and fennel sausages
600 g lean minced beef or veal
250 ml white wine
2 kg canned Italian tomatoes, squashed with your hands
6 bay leaves

To make the pastry, pour the flour onto a large surface and make a well in the middle. Add the softened butter to the well and amalgamate slowly, gradually adding the cold water. Season with salt and pepper, then knead gently for 5 minutes. Cover with plastic film, then rest in the fridge overnight.

To make the ragu sauce, heat the oil in a large heavy-based saucepan or flameproof casserole dish over medium heat, add the onion and cook until golden. Add the pork rib strips and cook until browned. Drain off the oil, reserving the onion and meat, then add the sausages and minced beef or veal and cook until nicely browned. Pour in the wine and boil over high heat until it has evaporated. Add the canned tomatoes and bring to the boil, then throw in the bay leaves. Reduce the heat and simmer for 2 hours. Set aside to cool.

This is a wee bit fiddly but important: when the ragu sauce has cooled, carefully remove the sausage skins (they will come away easily) with clean hands, then using a knife and fork cut the bones from the pork rib strips.

Preheat the oven to 160°C (fan-forced). Grease and flour a 23 cm round cake tin. Take the pastry out of the fridge and let it rest at room temperature for 10 minutes. Remove one quarter of the dough and set aside. On a floured surface, roll out the remaining dough to double the tin size (it has to line the entire tin with a little extra draped over the sides). The pastry should be no more than 1 cm thick.

Meanwhile, cook the rigatoni in boiling salted water for 12 minutes or until very al dente. Drain and mix well in a bowl with half the ragu. Take out the bay leaves, then add pepper (and salt if needed) and stir through half the parmesan. Pour into the pastry case, then roll out the reserved pastry and place gently over the top. Make a 3 cm hole in the middle, then pinch the edges together to seal. Brush with the beaten egg, then bake for 1 hour or until golden.

When the pie is just about ready, warm the remaining ragu. Serve in a bowl on the side, along with the remaining parmesan, so your guests can help themselves. This is a hearty 'bear wrestling' dish not to be messed with!

SECONDI

CHICKEN BREAST WITH BELL PEPPERS AND OLIVES

PETTO DI POLLO CON PEPERONI E OLIVE

by Anna Tizani

These chicken breasts are bursting with flavour, yet are super simple and lightning fast to prepare. If you get your two pans going at the same time, as I've seen Anna do, the entire dish is ready to eat in less than 20 minutes! Just keep the salt at a minimum – the capers and olives will most likely add all the saltiness you need.

SERVES 4

4 × 125 g chicken breast fillets, slightly flattened but not paper thin
plain flour, for dusting
salt and pepper
100 ml extra virgin olive oil, plus extra to serve
20 g butter
juice of ½ lemon, or to taste
2 medium red bell peppers, seeded and cut into thin strips
50 g green olives, pitted and thinly sliced
2 tablespoons salted capers, rinsed and drained
1 clove garlic, peeled and left whole
1–2 tablespoons torn basil leaves

Dust the chicken breasts with flour, shaking off any excess, and lightly season with salt. Heat 3 tablespoons oil in a large frying pan over medium heat and cook the breasts for 3 minutes, turning them once. Reduce the heat to low and add the butter and lemon juice, then cover and cook gently for a further 5 minutes, turning once.

Heat the remaining oil in a separate frying pan over medium–low heat and add the bell pepper, olives, capers, garlic clove and basil. Taste for salt and add if necessary, then cover and cook for 12–13 minutes, adding a little warm water if the mixture starts to dry out. Remove the garlic clove.

Serve the chicken breasts with the vegetables on the side or as a topping. This dish should be eaten while it's nice and hot, so serve immediately, with a final splash of oil.

Generally speaking, this is a dish prepared at home by the locals. Anna's recipe is outstanding and, like so many good wild meats, home-grown or organic rabbit gives a much better result. I think of this as a great winter meal, but I have seen plenty of semi-naked Italians tuck into dishes like this while sitting in sweltering conditions by the sea!

SERVES 6

50 g dried porcini mushrooms
1 tablespoon white wine vinegar
salt and pepper
1 kg small potatoes, peeled and left whole
90 ml extra virgin olive oil
1 small leek, white part only, washed and sliced
½ red bell pepper, seeded and diced
8 basil leaves, roughly chopped
1 thyme sprig, leaves picked and roughly chopped,
   plus extra sprigs to garnish
1 marjoram sprig, leaves picked and roughly chopped
80 g fresh breadcrumbs made from stale bread (see page 30)
1 egg
1.5 kg rabbit, boned (ask you butcher to do this for you)
1 rosemary sprig, leaves picked
1 onion, sliced
1 stick celery, sliced
2 carrots, sliced
250 ml white wine
2 teaspoons plain flour (optional)

Soak the porcini mushrooms in cold water for 1–2 hours or until soft. Rinse well and finely slice.

Bring a large saucepan of water to the boil and add the vinegar and plenty of salt. Add the potatoes and boil for 10–15 minutes or until tender.

Preheat the oven to 240°C (fan-forced).

Meanwhile, heat 1 tablespoon oil in a large frying pan over high heat, add the sliced mushroom, leek and bell pepper and cook, stirring, until caramelised. Season with salt and pepper then, when the vegetables are almost cooked, stir in the basil, thyme and marjoram. Transfer to a large bowl, then add the breadcrumbs and egg and mix to combine.

Spread your rabbit out on a board, skin-side down. Cover evenly with the vegetable stuffing, then firmly roll up the rabbit to enclose the stuffing. Secure with kitchen string, then place in a roasting tin, seam-side up (so you don't lose any juices) and drizzle with the remaining oil. Season with salt, pepper and rosemary

Bake for 20 minutes, then remove from the oven and reduce the heat to 190°C. Add the potato, onion, celery and carrot, then pour over the wine and bake for another 40 minutes.

Remove the rabbit and let it rest for a few minutes, then cut into thick slices. Serve on a bed of carrot, onion and celery, surrounded by the potatoes. Drizzle over the pan juices and serve garnished with extra thyme sprigs.

Alternatively, if you want to make a gravy, remove the potatoes and rabbit from the roasting tin and place on a warmed serving plate. Transfer the remaining vegetables and pan juices to a blender and blend until smooth. Return the puree to the roasting tin, add the flour and 125 ml water and cook, stirring, over high heat until reduced to a creamy gravy.

RABBIT INVOLTINI

INVOLTINI DI CONIGLIO

by Anna Tizani

RABBIT IS MY FAVOURITE MEAT, NEXT TO QUAIL, WHICH IS RARELY FOUND IN THIS AREA. HOWEVER, RABBIT IS MUCH EASIER TO LOCATE, ESPECIALLY IN THE MORE MOUNTAINOUS REGIONS OF THE COAST, AND WHEN A RESTAURANT OFFERS RABBIT IT MEANS THEY KNOW HOW TO COOK IT !

THREE-EGG EASTER GOAT

CAPRETTO ALL'UOVO

by Mario Rispoli

Mario's mother-in-law, Angela, was one of the best primary-school teachers I have ever known. She was the model of patience with her little terrors (including my son Marco) and always smiling. Sadly, she passed away at the end of 2010 and will be sadly missed in the small town of Positano, especially at Easter when she would prepare this unusual Easter goat. It's not a pretty dish (scrambled egg with meaty chunks!), but the flavour will always give it a number one vote!

SERVES 4

2 kg baby goat, cut into 3–4 cm pieces on the bone
   (ask your butcher to do this)
2 lemons, cut into quarters
juice of 4 lemons
200 ml extra virgin olive oil
4 medium brown onions, thinly sliced
200 ml white wine
salt
6 eggs
60 g parmesan, grated
coarsely grated pecorino, to serve
finely chopped flat-leaf parsley, to garnish

Place the goat pieces in a large saucepan and cover well with cold water. Add the lemon quarters and three-quarters of the lemon juice and leave to soak for 3 hours. Remove and pat dry.

Heat the oil in a large heavy-based frying pan or flameproof casserole dish large enough to fit the goat in one layer. Add the onion and cook over medium heat until lightly golden, then add the goat pieces and wine. Increase the heat and boil for about 5 minutes until the wine has evaporated, then season with salt. Reduce the heat to medium and cook, covered, for 1½ hours, turning the goat from time to time.

Meanwhile, beat the eggs with the parmesan, remaining lemon juice and a little salt.

When the goat is ready, pull away all the meat with a knife and fork and break it up into bite-sized pieces. Return the meat to the pan. Add the egg mix and stir constantly until the egg is cooked.

Spoon into shallow bowls and sprinkle with parmesan and pecorino. This is delicious served with fresh peas!

NOTE *According to Mario, the goats we purchase today from the butcher are mostly farmed and not wild, so the meat is more tender. However, if you do happen to acquire a wild goat (great for that extra flavour) a good way to make it tender is to freeze it before preparing the dish. The meat should fall off the bone.*

Mario's father-in-law, Bruno

Mario RISPOLI

POSITANO, RESTAURANT OWNER AND CHEF

Mario is one of the gentlest souls I've ever known. He quietly goes about his business in one of the smallest kitchens on the Amalfi Coast and I've never seen him lose his cool when the heat's on. He always has a smile on his face when I pop my head through the door of the Bar Bruno kitchen to see what's cooking for lunch.

I've known Mario and his dynamic wife Ornella since I opened my little T-shirt shop next door way back in the early 1990s. Back then, Bar Bruno was a snack bar run by Ornella's father, big ol' teddy bear Bruno. When Bruno passed away, Ornella and Mario took up the snack bar rent to stop anyone else from snatching up this great venue with the best view in town. They decided a trattoria might work better and that first summer employed a chef to cook up steaming bowls of pasta. But when the chef up and left halfway through August (the busiest month of the season and the time most chefs melt down), Mario had to throw on an apron and start cooking.

Mario grew up watching his capable mother cook family meals and she taught him the many basics he knows today. Unfortunately, when he opened the trattoria with the professional chef, he was waiting tables and never saw how anything was prepared. Disaster! He shyly confesses today that he thought gnocchi was cooked in the sauce and that it wasn't necessary to boil it first. It was certainly trial and error for that first season.

Mario's motto is 'Always use the freshest ingredients possible', and with the tiniest kitchen on the coast he's always had to buy fresh produce daily. What a bonus for us! His eventual aim is to increase the size of his cooking area, but he says he's content to cook in his matchbox kitchen for now.

Like many local boys, Mario has always loved the sea and even before he started cooking professionally, he was always passionate about cooking fresh fish at home. Today, fifteen years after opening his eatery, Mario is one of the region's finest and most naturally gifted chefs, loved and admired by locals and tourists alike for his unique flair with local produce and his passion for sharing that gift with us. Aren't we lucky?

MARIO'S RECIPES

ADA (BACK LEFT) WITH HUSBAND PEPPE
AND HER 'GORGEOUS BEACH BOYS'

Ada D'URZO

POSITANO, RESTAURATEUR AND COOK

Ada is a Minori native but after nearly three decades of life on the beach in Positano, it's hard to tell – she's a very well-known local face. It's almost twenty years since she and her husband Peppe set up a little snack and drinks bar on stilts on the beach at Arienzo, nestled under the splendid holiday villas of the rich and famous.

Arienzo beach is a classic Italian holiday dream, with crystal-clear waters, easy access to the town, a low-flying sociable duck that visits daily but never ends up in Ada's pot and, of course, Ada's wonderful food when it's time for lunch.

Initially, Peppe and Ada served only cold snacks, but after a year in business Ada carved a small kitchen out of the rock face flanking the beach. Here she started to prepare full restaurant-style dishes, from delectable homemade pastas to light grilled fish and salads. She'd always wanted to be a cook and, with three brothers who were professional cooks, it was inevitable.

Ada says her father was the true maestro in the kitchen while they were growing up and taught them everything they know. Her parmigiana di melanzane (eggplant parmigiana) is always a triumph, and the seaside guests line up for this dish every day during summer.

Thankfully, her daughter Amalia has also taken to the kitchen, creating delectable desserts. This little family business now has the perfect balance. Peppe runs a tight ship, looking after the guests, sorting out the splendidly manicured beach and its 200 beach beds and umbrellas, and making sure everyone gets on and off the boat safely when they arrive for a delicious meal. Aided by a small contingent of gorgeous beach boys, all of whom seem to be relatives, Ada is right where she wants to be – surrounded by family and cooking.

Now Ada has a new dream: she'd like to set up a winter cooking school at home, where tourists can learn the secrets of her kitchen. I'll be the first to book in!

ADA'S RECIPES

HUNTERS' CHICKEN

POLLO ALLA CACCIATORE

by Ada D'Urzo

This dish most likely originated in Tuscany and is commonly known as 'Hunters' chicken'. Ada's version is super non-fuss and works brilliantly. If you like a richer flavour, replace the white wine with an earthy red. To round out the meal, serve this with soft polenta, creamy mash or rice – it's not traditional, but it's a great combination.

SERVES 4

4 tablespoons extra virgin olive oil, plus extra to serve
1 large onion, roughly chopped
1–1.5 kg chicken, cut into pieces (or buy the same weight of chicken pieces)
250 ml white wine
10 cherry tomatoes, cut in half
1 rosemary sprig
1 marjoram sprig
salt and pepper

Gently heat the oil in a large heavy-based saucepan over low heat, add the onion and cook until transparent. Remove the onion and set aside. Increase the heat to medium, then add the chicken pieces and brown on all sides. Return the onion to the pan. Add the wine, tomatoes, rosemary, marjoram, salt and pepper, and any other vegetables you wish to add. Reduce the heat to low and cook, uncovered, for 1 hour, turning the chicken pieces occasionally.

This is a slightly different way of preparing alla cacciatore, which is nearly always covered for the final slow-cooking period, so keep a close eye on the liquid level. If it starts to dry out, add a little warm water.

Divide among four serving plates, drizzle with extra oil and serve hot.

NOTE *The choice of vegetables is very much up to you. Ada keeps it very simple but you can also add bell pepper and mushrooms, if you like. It is definitely a recipe that can be tailor-made to suit individual tastes.*

SECONDI

Although this dish is an antipasto, if the calamari is big enough it makes a great secondo. In the south of Italy it's unusual to combine cheese with seafood, but when it's the right seafood and the right cheese they can make a very happy couple. Roberto is known for his harmonious balance in the kitchen and, although practically EVERYTHING in his little trattoria has been hauled out of the sea, you will often find surprise ingredients that will give his dishes that little twist of originality. If your calamari have lovely long tentacles, keep a few aside to cook with the rest of the calamari, then use to decorate the plate.

STUFFED CALAMARI WITH POTATOES AND PROVOLA

CALAMARI IMBOTTITI DI PATATE E PROVOLA

by Roberto Proto

SERVES 6

1 medium potato
250 ml extra virgin olive oil
6 × 200 g calamari, cleaned, tentacles removed
  and cut into large pieces
salt
200 ml white wine
360 g provola cheese, finely chopped
pinch of freshly grated nutmeg
pinch of pepper
6 sprigs flat-leaf parsley, to garnish (optional)

Steam the potato in its skin until tender. Leave to cool slightly, then peel and roughly chop.

Heat 125 ml oil in a medium frying pan over medium–low heat, add the tentacles and salt and cook for 7 minutes. Take the pan off the heat and add the wine, then return to high heat and cook for 3 minutes or until the wine has evaporated. Pour in 125 ml water and bring to the boil, then reduce the heat to low and cook for 15 minutes or until all the liquid has evaporated. Set aside to cool.

Place the cooled potato, tentacles and provola in an electric mixer and mix to a rough paste. Season with nutmeg, pepper and salt, to taste.

Spoon the paste into the calamari tubes to about three-quarters full (or use a piping bag, if preferred), then secure with toothpicks. Take care not to overfill the calamari or the stuffing will leak out during cooking.

Heat the remaining oil in a large frying pan over medium heat, add the stuffed calamari and cook for about 3 minutes each side or until golden. Add 250 ml water and bring to the boil, then reduce the heat to very low and cook, covered, for 40 minutes. Check the water levels often and add a little hot water if it starts to dry out.

Remove the calamari from the pan and keep warm. Increase the heat under the cooking liquid and boil until reduced and creamy.

Serve the calamari whole or cut into 2 cm thick rounds. Pour the sauce over the top and garnish with parsley (if using) or lemon leaves, if you happen to have a lemon tree in your garden! Serve hot. Buon appetito!

IN THIS PART OF ITALY, PROVOLA AND PROVOLONE ARE FREQUENTLY FOUND IN THE KITCHEN AS THEY ARE PRODUCED JUST UP THE ROAD IN AGEROLA. IF ANY CHEESE IS USED WITH FISH, IT WILL MOST LIKELY BE THIS ONE.

BAKED COD WITH BABY CLAMS AND PEAS

MERLUZZO CON PISELLI E VONGOLE AL FORNO

by Erika Villani

For years I was lucky enough to live down the road from the Savino family's glamorous hillside restaurant. It was our first stop for a special meal with visiting friends and family. My step-brother (also Italian, a great gourmet and very fussy) came to visit many years ago and he sampled this signature dish at the restaurant. He declared it to be one of the best three he'd eaten anywhere in the world! It can be difficult to find small cod in Australia so while it looks amazing using a whole fish, I give the recipe here using cod fillets, which work just as well. Even Erika uses fillets when the restaurant is very busy!

SERVES 4

120 ml extra virgin olive oil
1 large clove garlic, finely chopped
800 g cod fillets
salt and pepper
250 g frozen peas (or fresh, if you have them)
40 baby clams, well purged of sand – these will give you the juice of this dish
1–2 tablespoons roughly chopped flat-leaf parsley
toasted ciabatta, to serve

Heat the oil in a large deep frying pan over medium heat, add the garlic and cook until golden. Reduce the heat to low, then add the cod fillets, a couple of teaspoons of salt and 1 litre hot water and simmer, covered, for 10 minutes. Add the peas and cook for another 5 minutes. If there is too much liquid, remove the lid and boil over high heat until most of the liquid has evaporated. You want to be left with a couple of tablespoons for each serve.

When the fish is cooked (check by inserting a knife in the thickest part of each fillet – if the flesh is white, it's ready), add the clams and cook, covered, over medium heat until they open (discard any that don't open). This should take about 3 minutes. Scatter over the parsley and serve with toasted ciabatta to soak up the glorious juices.

ERIKA'S FATHER, WHO IS THE MAITRE'D IN THE RESTAURANT, TOLD ME THAT WHEN HE OFFERS BAKED COD TO NEAPOLITAN CLIENTELE, THEY OFTEN REPLY, 'WHY WOULD I WANT COD? DO I LOOK ILL?' APPARENTLY IT IS THE CUSTOM IN SOME PARTS OF ITALY TO FEED THIS NUTRITIOUS WHITE-FLESHED FISH TO BEDRIDDEN HOSPITAL PATIENTS. IF THEY ONLY KNEW HOW DELICIOUS THIS RECIPE IS!

Many years ago Pasquale taught me how to prepare this dish and I have never eaten a better version in anyone's home or restaurant anywhere in the world. There are three little tricks: not too much egg white; use a mixture of rock salt and fine salt; and pack the salt mixture over the fish with wet hands. When you have mastered these, the rest is as easy as falling off a log and the result is infallible!

SERVES 6

1.25 kg rock salt
1.25 kg fine salt
3 egg whites, whipped to soft peaks
2 × 1.5 kg white fish (preferably snapper), gutted but not scaled
mint leaves, to garnish

DRESSING

300 ml extra virgin olive oil
large handful of mint leaves, torn
aged balsamic vinegar or white vinegar, to taste
salt

Preheat the oven to 180°C (fan-forced).

To make the dressing, mix the ingredients together in a small bowl with a fork. Keep tasting and adjusting until you get the right balance. If using good-quality balsamic, you probably only need a drop or two.

Mix the two salts together and fold in the egg white. Spread a thin layer of the salt mix onto a large baking tray then place the two fish on top (side by side, head to tail). Pour the remaining salt mix over the top and, with slightly damp hands, pack the salt down onto the fish, being careful to seal every hole – you don't want to see one scale poking through. Perhaps the tail can poke out, but not the head!

Bake for 30–40 minutes (about 30 minutes per kilogram is the general rule). The salt crust will be lovely and golden when ready.

Using a kitchen hammer and knife, crack the crust near the fish shoulder (do this somewhere in the kitchen or garden where you don't mind a little mess as the crust will be very hard!). Check the fish is cooked through (pop it back in the oven if not), then crack the rest of the crust open. The skin (with scales) should come away in one large peel after you have removed the salt crust. Plate up as quickly as you can so the fish doesn't get too cold, then drizzle with the mint dressing. Serve garnished with mint leaves.

NOTES *You get much better results if you cook two smaller fish rather than one big one. For this reason, I never cook this recipe with fish larger than 1.5 kg.*

If you have a super aged balsamic, forget the dressing and add just a few drops to each portion of fish, along with a mint leaf or two – nothing else. Buon appetito!

INFALLIBLE BAKED FISH UNDER SALT!

PESCE SOTTO IL SALE

by Pasquale Marino

LIFE ON THE AMALFI COAST IS INCREDIBLY SPONTANEOUS. MEALS ARE CREATED ACCORDING TO WHAT LOOKS GOOD AT THE MARKET, AND THERE ALWAYS SEEMS TO BE AN EXCITING SURPRISE WAITING FOR YOU, SUCH AS A SUDDEN DECISION TO JUMP ON A BOAT AT SUNSET AND HEAD UP THE COAST FOR A BEACH SUPPER. THIS 'ESPRESSO' LIFESTYLE IS WHAT MADE ME FALL IN LOVE WITH THIS PART OF THE WORLD.

CITIES ALL OVER THE WORLD ARE FULL OF THE REVAMPED FIAT CINQUECENTO (500). BUT IF YOU WANT TO SEE THE 'REAL DEAL' YOU WON'T HAVE TO LOOK FAR ON THE AMALFI COAST - THEY ARE EVERYWHERE! THIS CAR WAS <u>BUILT</u> FOR THIS AREA, WHICH IS TIGHT WITH LIMITED SPACE, WINDY ROADS AND LITTLE PARKING. THEY LAST FOREVER, SO ARE HANDED DOWN FROM GENERATION TO GENERATION. THIS LITTLE CAR IS SO LOVED AND SO WELL LOOKED AFTER - IT'S QUITE TOUCHING REALLY.

BAKED SALMON FANS

SALMONE A VENTAGLIO

by Mena Vanacore

Salmon is not commonly found on the Amalfi Coast but, like most things from the sea in this part of the world, when you do find it, it's delicious. Made with local ingredients to enhance the salmon flavour, this must be the quickest secondo you will ever prepare, but there's a reason for that: you need the extra time for Mena's mind-blowing almond chocolate cake! See page 208 for the recipe.

SERVES 6

6 slices 2-day-old ciabatta, crusts removed
1 teaspoon salted capers, rinsed and drained
3 large flat-leaf parsley leaves
1 slice garlic
1 tablespoon extra virgin olive oil
6 × 200 g salmon fillets, skin on
garden salad, to serve

HERB DRESSING

90 ml extra virgin olive oil
pinch of salt
1 tablespoon lemon juice
6 large flat-leaf parsley leaves, roughly chopped
6 large mint leaves, roughly chopped

Place the bread, capers, parsley and garlic in a blender and pulse three or four times just to break up the bread. Stir in the oil by hand. Leave to marinate for at least 30 minutes.

Preheat the oven to 200°C (fan-forced). Line a baking dish with baking paper. Place the salmon fillets on a board, skin-side down, and make slits going in the opposite direction to its length right down to the skin, 1 cm apart. Cover the salmon flesh with the bread mixture, right into the slits. Leave the skin side uncoated.

Place the salmon in the baking dish, skin-side down, and bake on the middle rack for 15 minutes, checking regularly.

Meanwhile, to make the herb dressing, mix the ingredients together in a small bowl with a spoon or fork.

Remove the salmon from the oven and drizzle with the dressing while still hot, making sure you pour some into the slits which will have opened during cooking. Serve with a fresh garden salad.

FRIED FLYING SQUID AND POTATOES ALLA PRAIANESE

TOTANI E PATATE FRITTE ALLA PRAIANESE

by Felice Fiore

This is the 'other' version of Flying squid and potatoes (see also page 183). The tradition in Praiano has always been to fry their squid and potato, whereas in Positano and other coastal areas, it is often found in the form of a stew. This is quick and light to prepare and Felice is genuinely brilliant at it.

SERVES 6

500 ml peanut oil
1 kg pontiac potatoes, cut into 1 cm thick wedges
125 ml extra virgin olive oil
1 medium onion, thinly sliced
1 hot chilli, finely chopped (optional)
1 kg red squid, well cleaned, tentacles removed
    and chopped, tubes cut into rings
salt
flat-leaf parsley leaves, to garnish
lemon wedges, to serve (optional)

Heat the peanut oil in a large deep frying pan until very hot but not smoking, add the potato wedges and cook until golden and cooked through. Remove and drain on paper towels.

Heat the olive oil in a large heavy-based frying pan over medium heat, add the onion and chilli (if using) and cook until the onion is transparent. Add the squid pieces. Reduce the heat and cook, tossing, for 1 minute, then cover and cook for 5–10 minutes until the squid is nicely coloured and tender.

Add the potato wedges to the squid and toss together well. Remove from the heat, season with salt and sprinkle with parsley. Serve immediately with lemon wedges, if liked.

THE FIRST TIME I EVER HAD SUNDAY LUNCH WITH FELICE'S FAMILY, SHE TOLD ME WE WOULD BE EATING `TOTANI E PATATE', BUT I WAS TOTALLY UNPREPARED FOR WHAT SHE THEN PRESENTED AT THE TABLE. MEMBERS OF HER EXTENSIVE FAMILY HAVE DIFFERENT PREFERENCES — SOME LIKE IT FRIED, OTHERS PREFER IT STEWED, AND SOME LIKE IT WITHOUT TOMATO. SO FELICE PREPARES ALL THREE VERSIONS TO KEEP THE ENTIRE FAMILY HAPPY. NOW THAT'S A DEDICATED COOK!

Is there a country in the world that doesn't have its own version of meatloaf? I doubt it. Consiglia's meatloaf is truly Neapolitan, full of flavour and laden with hearty ingredients. Any leftovers become a tasty sandwich filling the next day or the base for a delicious pasta sauce the following evening.

SERVES 6–8

200 g centre dough of stale bread (no crust)
300 ml milk
900 g minced meat (beef, pork or veal, or a combination)
3 eggs
100 g parmesan, grated
1 clove garlic, finely chopped
1–2 tablespoons finely chopped flat-leaf parsley
salt and pepper
100 g sliced ham
2 eggs, extra, boiled and peeled
large splash of extra virgin olive oil
2 carrots, chopped
1 stick celery, chopped
1 small white onion, chopped
125 ml white wine
250 ml beef stock

TOMATO SAUCE

2½ tablespoons extra virgin olive oil
½ white onion, finely chopped
1 × 400 g can Italian tomatoes
5 basil leaves
salt

Preheat the oven to 180°C (fan-forced).

Soak the bread in the milk, then squeeze dry, discarding the milk. Combine the bread with the minced meat, then add the eggs, parmesan, garlic, parsley, salt and pepper. Mix well with your hands, then transfer to a large sheet of baking paper and spread out to form a large rectangle. Spread the ham over the mince mixture, then place the boiled eggs in the middle. With the help of the baking paper, roll up the mince mixture into a long sausage, then twist the ends like a large lolly. Carefully unroll the paper and transfer the meatloaf to a baking dish. Add a splash of oil and the carrot, celery, onion, wine and stock and bake for for 1¼–1½ hours or until cooked through.

Meanwhile, to make the sauce, heat the oil in a small heavy-based saucepan over medium heat. Add the onion and cook until transparent, then add the tomatoes and reduce the heat to low. Add the basil leaves and salt to taste, then simmer gently for 30 minutes.

Remove the meatloaf from the oven and rest for 5–10 minutes. Cut into thick slices and serve with the warm tomato sauce.

POLPETTE NAPOLETANO

by Consiglia Giudone

OVEN-BAKED WHOLE FISH IN WHITE WINE

PESCE AL FORNO CON VINO BIANCO

by Aldo Caso

A whole fresh fish in a light creamy sauce is my idea of bliss at the table, and there's not a drop of cream in this recipe! Soaking up the appetising sauce with a piece of fresh local bread (similar to a good ciabatta) really sets off the delicate flavour of the fish. I've been begging Aldo for this recipe for years, and finally here it is!

SERVES 6

6 × 250–300 g white fish (preferably snapper,
   otherwise grey mullet or whiting), scaled and gutted
plain flour, for dusting
salt and pepper
100 ml extra virgin olive oil
1 clove garlic, peeled and squashed
500 g small pontiac potatoes, peeled and thinly sliced
250 ml dry white wine
2 tablespoons torn flat-leaf parsley
500 ml good-quality fish stock, plus extra if needed
   (see 94 if you want to make your own)
flat-leaf parsley sprigs and cherry tomatoes, to garnish (optional)

Preheat the oven to 200°C (fan-forced).

Lightly coat the fish in seasoned flour, shaking off any excess.

Heat the oil in a large flameproof baking dish or tin over medium heat. Add the garlic clove and cook until golden. Remove the garlic. Add the fish, then turn them over immediately. Add the potato and toss to coat in the oil, then pour in the wine and let it boil rapidly over high heat until it has evaporated. Stir in the parsley.

Add the stock, then turn the fish over. Transfer to the oven and bake for 10–15 minutes, basting two or three times and adding more stock if it starts to dry out. Pull away a fish bone from shoulder area – if it comes away easily, the fish is ready. Serve the fish and potatoes, drizzled with the cooking juices. Garnish with parsley sprigs and cherry tomatoes, if liked.

I don't believe there is a household, decent deli or restaurant on the Amalfi Coast that does not offer this dish, but Ada's version is particularly well regarded. It is a staple offering at her beachside restaurant and customers line up for it! The trick is to maintain the rich flavours without letting the dish become too oily. The smell of it cooking attracts people from all over town – it is a true culinary delight.

EGGPLANT BAKE

PARMIGIANA DI MELANZANE

by Ada D'Urzo

SERVES 6

1.5 kg medium eggplants (aubergines), cut into 5 mm thick slices
salt
1 litre peanut oil
100 ml extra virgin olive oil (or less if you want a lighter dish)
1 clove garlic, peeled and left whole
1.5 kg good-quality canned Italian tomatoes
500 g day-old mozzarella, cut into 2 cm dice (not buffalo mozzarella
  as it contains too much water and will flood your dish)
1 bunch basil, leaves torn
grated parmesan, for sprinkling

Place the eggplant slices in a large colander, sprinkle with 1 tablespoon salt and leave for 30 minutes. Rinse well and pat dry with paper towels.

Heat the peanut oil in a large frying pan over high heat until hot but not smoking, add the eggplant slices (in batches if necessary) and cook until golden on both sides. Drain on paper towel in a colander for 2 hours (if possible), changing the paper towel when it becomes saturated to make sure as much oil as possible is removed.

Meanwhile, heat the olive oil in a large frying pan over low heat, add the garlic clove and cook until golden. Remove the garlic. Add the canned tomatoes and some salt and cook over medium–low heat for 30 minutes.

Preheat the oven to 180°C (fan-forced).

Cover the bottom of a large baking dish with a thin layer of tomato sauce then add alternate layers of eggplant, mozzarella and tomato sauce, with a layer of basil in the middle. Finish with a layer of tomato sauce, then scatter over a generous amount of parmesan. The thickness of your parmigiana will depend on the size of the dish – the smaller the dish, the more layers you will have.

Bake for about 15 minutes (more if you have many layers – you want the mozzarella to melt all the way through). Remove from the oven and rest for 10 minutes before serving.

THE ORIGINS OF THIS RECIPE ARE DEFINITELY FROM CAMPANIA, AND IT HAS BEEN AROUND FOR AT LEAST 200 YEARS. ALL THE INGREDIENTS IN THIS DELICIOUS CREATION ARE WIDELY USED IN THIS AREA, FROM THE SILKEN EGGPLANT TO THE SWEET TOMATOES AND MOZZARELLA CHEESE. I NOTICED THE LABOURERS AROUND POSITANO WOULD OFTEN STUFF A LARGE CHUNK OF PIZZA DOUGH BREAD WITH PARMIGIANA DI MELANZANE AND HAVE IT FOR LUNCH!

RABBIT WITH HERB CRUST BAKED ON LEMON LEAVES

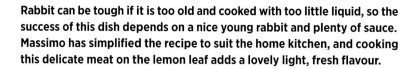

CONIGLIO CON LA CROSTA DI ERBE 'SULLE FOGLIE DI LIMONE

by Massimo Proto

Rabbit can be tough if it is too old and cooked with too little liquid, so the success of this dish depends on a nice young rabbit and plenty of sauce. Massimo has simplified the recipe to suit the home kitchen, and cooking this delicate meat on the lemon leaf adds a lovely light, fresh flavour.

SERVES 6

1.2 kg young rabbit
juice of 2 lemons
3 eggs, lightly beaten
2 tablespoons finely chopped aromatic herbs (such as rosemary, thyme, sage and oregano), plus extra herbs for lining the dish
20 g pecorino, grated
salt
300 g fresh breadcrumbs made from stale bread (see page 30)
50 g butter, plus extra if needed
1 tablespoon extra virgin olive oil, plus extra if needed
about 30 large lemon leaves, well washed and patted dry

Cut the rabbit into pieces about the size of a tennis ball (bone in). Rinse under running water, then place in a large bowl and pour over the lemon juice. Leave for at least 1 hour, tossing every so often to release all the wild flavours. Rinse the rabbit pieces and pat dry with paper towels.

Preheat the oven to 180°C (fan-forced).

Combine the egg, herbs, pecorino and salt in a bowl, add the rabbit pieces and toss with your hands to coat. Marinate for about 5 minutes, then coat in the breadcrumbs.

Melt the butter and oil in a large frying pan over medium–high heat and brown the rabbit pieces for 3 minutes each side. Add a little more butter or oil if needed.

Line a baking dish with lemon leaves and extra herbs then place the rabbit pieces on top. Scatter more lemon leaves over the rabbit, then cover the dish with a lid or foil and bake for 35 minutes. If the breadcrumbs are a little soggy, take off the lid and increase the heat to 250°C. Let the crumbs crisp up for 5 minutes or so.

Your end result should be a juicy, succulent and flavoursome bunny! Great with mash or baked smashed potatoes.

ACCORDING TO MASSIMO, THE BEST RABBITS ARE FROM THE 'FOODIE' ISLAND OF NEARBY ISCHIA, WHERE THIS RECIPE IS FROM.

This very traditional dish is one of Rosetta's prize recipes. I believe she has cooked more flying squid and potato stew than most of us have had breakfasts! The squid in this area are exceptional, as are the potatoes, so this dish is a winner before she even starts cooking. It is just too good to pass up if you see it on a menu, even on the beach in 40°C heat!

FLYING SQUID AND POTATO STEW

TOTANI E PATATE (IN UMIDO)

by Rosetta D'Urso

SERVES 6

100 ml extra virgin olive oil
1 large clove garlic, finely chopped
1 small brown onion, finely chopped
½ hot chilli, finely chopped
1 kg very fresh squid, well cleaned, tentacles removed
   and chopped, tubes cut into rings
6 small cherry tomatoes, cut into quarters
2–3 tablespoons roughly chopped flat-leaf parsley, plus extra to garnish
700 g pontiac potatoes, cut into thin wedges.
salt
warm ciabatta, to serve

Heat the oil in a large deep frying pan with a lid over medium–low heat, add the garlic, onion and chilli and cook until golden. Add the squid rings and tentacles and cook for about 15 minutes or until golden. Stir in the tomato and parsley and cook for 5 minutes, then add the potato.

Add 500 ml water and pinch of salt, then cover and cook over low heat for 30 minutes or until the squid is tender. If it is still a bit tough, cook for a little while longer. Remove from the heat and leave to rest, covered, for 10 minutes. Sprinkle with extra parsley and serve with warm ciabatta to soak up the yummy juices.

NOTE *You can cook this a few hours in advance, if you like, then gently warm through for 10 minutes over low heat.*

EVERY YEAR I'D DESIGN A DIFFERENT T-SHIRT FOR DA ADOLFO RISTORANTE, USUALLY BASED ON WHAT CAME FROM THE SEA IN THE AMALFI AREA — GENERALLY WHAT YOU'D BE SERVED FOR LUNCH! I CREATED THIS FLYING SQUID IMAGE THE THIRD OR FOURTH YEAR I WAS THERE, AND IT WAS VERY WELL RECEIVED BY OUR LOCAL CLIENTELE BECAUSE TO CALL SOMEONE A 'TOTONO' (SQUID) IN NEAPOLITAN IS AN AFFECTIONATE WAY OF CALLING THEM AN IDIOT!

Erminia CUOMO

FURORE , RESTAURANT CHEF

Erminia is the wife of Furore's mayor Raffaele Ferraioli, who has to be one of the Amalfi Coast's most dedicated and respected mayors. More importantly for us, she's a wonderful cook and has worked in Raffaele's family restaurant, Il Bacco, for more than forty years. It wouldn't be the same without her.

As the first of twelve children, Erminia made her debut in the kitchen at the ripe age of nine. She had a pretty full-on childhood, assisting her mother in caring for her younger siblings, so by the time she met and married Raffaele Ferraioli at twenty-one, she was well and truly ready to move on. At the time, Raffaele owned a little mountaintop restaurant called Il Bacco, and the capable Erminia immediately found herself back in the kitchen. As Erminia says, she went from la padella alla brace (the fat to the fire). Today, after forty-three years of hard work, she has no intention of giving away any of her kitchen duties. She's totally dedicated to her work with food, creating everything from simple delicious meals using the wonderful local produce of Furore to more complicated traditional dishes worshipped by locals and travellers alike.

She and her sister-in-law Rosa also run the hotel side of the business, cleaning it daily from top to bottom, servicing and maintaining the rooms, and feeding the guests, not to mention running their own families. Il Bacco has been recommended by numerous international food guides over the years, including the famous Italian Slow Food.

Consiglia GIUDONE

POSITANO, PRIVATE VILLA CHEF , HEAD HOTEL MAID AND JACK OF ALL TRADES

Consiglia has a look that says, 'Don't mess with me.' This is a good thing, as over the years she's cooked for Russian royalty, Hollywood film crews, world-famous singers and captains of industry. But nothing fazes Consiglia: when she's in her kitchen she reigns supreme and is in total control – not bad for a woman who's only been cooking professionally for five years.

Baking cakes has been her passion since she was a small girl, and eventually became her profession. She's travelled miles to attend good cooking schools, courses and workshops, with plenty of practice for friends and family in between.

Consiglia is an all-rounder in the restaurant. Hotels and restaurants looking for the best kitchen staff generally opt for strong young boys who can lift heavy cases of wine and sacks of flour. Consiglia has the strength of a seasoned athlete, having worked for years as a head hotel maid and lifted more furniture and mattresses than most of us have lifted knives and forks. There's little she can't tackle. She's one of those cooks who'll always find a few extra hours in the day, whipping up goodies for one of the local delis or a gourmet takeaway.

I sometimes spot her around town on a motorbike with her husband Pasquale, with whom I waited tables down by the sea many moons ago. When I jokingly ask him if he's cooking for the family these days, Consiglia always jumps to his defence, saying he cooks a mean pasta aglio e olio. I love these dedicated southern Italian women!

Consiglia's dream is to work in an upmarket restaurant one day – 'the ones where you never see women in the kitchen,' she says. I reckon she'd give any Michelin-starred cook a run for their money!

This light secondo has to be one of the quickest, yummiest dishes on the run. The entire process takes less than 15 minutes and the flavour is amazing. The trick is to find really fresh wild fennel seeds and a rich balsamic vinegar (you don't need much, but the flavour lingers). I love eating these dishes at Erminia's as they leave plenty of room for all the other goodies.

WHITE FISH FILLETS WITH WILD FENNEL

FILETTO DI PESCE CON FINOCCHIETTO SELVATICO

by Erminia Cuomo

SERVES 6

100 ml extra virgin olive oil
3 tablespoons white wine
6 fish fillets (john dory is perfect)
1 teaspoon finocchietto (wild fennel seeds), finely chopped
    (use ground fennel seeds if unavailable)
fresh breadcrumbs made from stale bread (see page 30),
    for sprinkling
salt
3 teaspoons good balsamic vinegar
fennel fronds, to garnish

Preheat the oven to 200°C (fan-forced).

Combine the oil and wine in a baking dish large enough to fit the fish fillets in a single layer. Add the fillets, then sprinkle with the chopped wild fennel seeds, breadcrumbs, salt and ½ teaspoon balsamic vinegar for each fillet.

Cover and bake for 10 minutes or until the breadcrumbs are lightly golden. Uncover and cook for a further 2 minutes to crisp them up. Garnish with fennel fronds and serve immediately.

FINOCCHIETTO IS WILD FENNEL THAT GROWS ABUNDANTLY ON THE AMALFI COAST. IT CAN BE FOUND GROWING WILD IN AUSTRALIA IN UNEXPECTED PLACES SUCH AS CENTENNIAL PARK IN SYDNEY!

BAKED BABY GOAT WITH SAME-JUICE POTATOES

CAPRETTO AL FORNO

by Daniele Bella

According to the great food historian of the Amalfi Coast, sadly and recently deceased Ezio Falcone, goat is the most widely eaten meat in this area, with pork and rabbit running a close second. You will not find goat on too many menus, but if you are around these parts during Easter, you will smell it baking away happily in many home kitchens. It is one of my favourites, and we would often cook half a goat in our living-room fireplace on those chilly Easter Sundays. What a treat! You will need to soak the goat before cooking it, so start this recipe at least a day ahead.

SERVES 8

200 ml white vinegar
2.75 litres white wine, plus extra if needed
1 bunch rosemary, leaves picked
2 onions, diced
2 carrots, diced
70 g salt
2 large goat shoulders, bone in
2 onions, extra, sliced
150 g dried black olives
1 kg pontiac potatoes, peeled and cut into 2 cm dice
100 ml extra virgin olive oil

Combine the vinegar, 2 litres wine, half the rosemary leaves, the diced onion and carrot and 50 g salt in a large non-metallic container. Add the goat pieces and marinate in the fridge for 24 hours, turning them halfway through. Remove the goat and pat dry with paper towels.

Preheat the oven to 200°C (fan-forced).

Place the goat pieces in a large heavy baking dish. Add the sliced onion, olives, potato, oil, remaining wine, remaining rosemary and remaining salt and toss together well.

Bake for 30 minutes, then reduce the heat to 180°C and cook for another 2½ hours. Turn the goat pieces every 30 minutes or so, and check the liquid – if it appears dry, add a little mixture of equal parts water and wine. Remove the goat and rest for 10 minutes before serving.

YEARS LATER, WHEN I MOVED BACK TO AUSTRALIA AND NO LONGER HAD AN OPEN FIREPLACE, I MADE SURE WHEN RENOVATING MY KITCHEN THAT MY OVEN WAS WIDE ENOUGH TO ACCOMMODATE HALF A BABY GOAT. HOWEVER, HOT WEATHER AND BAKED GOAT JUST DON'T SEEM TO GO TOGETHER, SO I AM STILL FANTASISING ABOUT IT. PERHAPS IN THE SPRING ...

COD WITH DRIED FISH ROE

MERLUZZO con LA BOTTARGA

by Gennaro Marciante

The last time I visited Gennaro in his small but super-professional kitchen in Cetara, I watched him prepare this dish while we enjoyed literally two sips of wine. That's how quick it is to make! A quick flash in the pan for the cod, squeeze the potato through a ricer, a drizzle of extra virgin olive oil and the final flourish of grated dried fish roe. What an explosion of flavour!

SERVES 6

600 g pontiac potatoes
6 cod fillets, skin and bones removed
120 ml extra virgin olive oil
180 g dried red fish roe
1–2 teaspoons finely chopped flat-leaf parsley (optional)

Boil the potatoes in their skins until tender (don't salt the water). Drain and leave to cool slightly, then peel.

Meanwhile, place the cod fillets in a medium frying pan with 2 litres water, bring to the boil and cook for 5 minutes.

Divide the cod fillets among six plates, then, using a ricer, squeeze a good amount of potato onto each fillet. Drizzle a tablespoon of oil over each serve, then finish with a generous grating of dried fish roe and a scattering of parsley (if using). Amazingly simple, amazingly good!

NOTE *Simplicity in the kitchen is great but the key is to make sure your ingredients are the best you can buy – especially that dried fish roe.*

BEAUTIFULLY PRESERVED BOTTARGA (FISH ROE), READY FOR GRATING

TRADITIONAL PASTA AND SAUSAGE BAKE

MIGLIACCIO DI FURORE

by Erminia Cuomo

Migliaccio is the typical dish of the town where Erminia lives, works and cooks – Furore. Naturally, every household has their own variation but the foundations are generally the same: pork sausage, pasta and semolina. Nice and hearty! Erminia is a champion at making this dish and if you follow her instructions below, you will be crying for a second slice . . . even though you won't know where to put it!

SERVES 4-6

salt
250 g Italian pork sausages with fennel
50 g ziti pasta
250 g semolina
50 g parmesan, grated
3 boiled eggs, cut into quarters
extra virgin olive oil, for cooking
fresh breadcrumbs made from stale bread (see page 30), for sprinkling

Bring 750 ml lightly salted water to the boil (you don't need much as the sausage is already salty). Add the sausages and boil for 10 minutes. Remove (reserving the water) and cool slightly, then take off the skins. Chop the sausage meat into bite-sized pieces, or just break it up with your fingers.

Bring the water back to the boil and cook the ziti pasta for 5 minutes until quite al dente, then whisk in the semolina and stir constantly with a wooden spoon for about 10 minutes or until the water has been absorbed. Remove the pan from the heat and add the sausage, parmesan and egg. Mix gently. If there is too much liquid, spoon out the excess before the end of the cooking time; if there is not enough, add some boiling water.

Lightly coat a medium deep ovenproof frying pan with oil, then sprinkle with breadcrumbs, shaking out any excess. Pack the semolina mixture into the pan and sprinkle more breadcrumbs over the top. Cook over low heat for about 10 minutes. Now you need to flip it over. The best way to do this is to cover the pan with a flat lid with a handle, tip the semolina bake onto the lid, then shuffle it back into the pan with the bottom-side now on the top. Sprinkle with more breadcrumbs if needed and cook for another 10 minutes. If you want the bake to be a deep golden colour, put the pan in a preheated 200°C (fan forced) oven and cook to the desired colour. Turn out and cool for 30 minutes before serving in generous wedges.

NOTE *If you like, stir in the traditional ingredients of 30 g raisins and 30 g pine nuts when you add the sausage to the semolina mix.*

SECONDI

VEAL FILLETS WITH MARJORAM

FILETTO
DI VITELLONE ALLA MAGGIORANA

by Erminia Cuomo

This cut of veal is often seen in Italy but it's not so common in Australia. If you don't have access to a good Italian butcher perhaps a simple description will be enough: they are fillets of baby beef (vitellone), cut about 1.5 cm thick (slightly thicker than scaloppine). They are full of flavour and take very little time to cook. Here Erminia serves this light veal dish with her fabulous homemade potato chips. Simple and appetising!

SERVES 6
300 ml extra virgin olive oil
3 tablespoons marjoram leaves
4 cloves garlic, finely chopped
fresh or dried chilli, to taste
6 fillets of baby beef or veal, cut 1.5 cm thick
fresh breadcrumbs made from stale bread (see page 30), for coating
salt
rosemary sprigs and lemon wedges, to serve (optional)

FRIED POTATO ROUNDS
3 medium pontiac potatoes, peeled and cut into thin slices (about 3–5 mm)
250 ml extra virgin olive oil
salt

Mix together the oil, marjoram, garlic and chilli in a large non-metallic dish. Remove half and reserve for later. Add the veal fillets to the remaining marinade and turn to coat. Set aside for 10–15 minutes.

To make the potato rounds, heat the oil in a large frying pan over high heat until very hot but not smoking. Gently slide in the potatoes and cook for 5–6 minutes or until golden on both sides. Depending on the size of your pan, you may need to cook them in batches. Drain quickly on paper towels, then season with salt and serve piping hot.

Meanwhile, heat a barbecue grill plate to low (use a heavy chargrill pan on the stove if you don't have a barbecue). Coat the veal in the breadcrumbs, shaking off any excess, then cook until lightly golden on both sides. You want them to be medium, not well done. Season with salt and serve with the fried potato rounds, rosemary sprigs and lemon wedges, if liked. Finish each serve with a drizzle of the reserved marinade.

KING PRAWNS WITH ROCKET AND BRANDY

GAMBERONI CON RUGHETTA E BRANDY

by Roberto Proto

Roberto has embraced the art of flambe in this recipe. Once a sign of great culinary prowess in the 1960s, this skill was generally exhibited by professional staff at the table in upmarket restaurants. Roberto prefers to perform his magic hidden away in the kitchen, but the flavours he brings to the plate are what matters. He frequently offers unusual twists to his dishes, and they are always beautifully balanced and much appreciated by locals and visiting clientele.

SERVES 6

125 ml extra virgin olive oil
1 clove garlic, peeled and left whole
1.5 kg king prawns (about 5 per person), peeled and deveined, head and tail intact
125 ml brandy
50 g rocket, finely chopped, plus extra leaves to garnish
salt

Heat the oil in a large frying pan over medium heat, add the garlic clove and cook until golden. Remove the garlic.

Take the pan off the heat and add the prawns, then return to high heat and cook for 2 minutes on each side.

Remove from the heat again and add the brandy, then return to high heat. The brandy should ignite briefly. Cover the pan with a lid to extinguish the flame, then add 125 ml water, the chopped rocket and some salt. Cook uncovered for 3 minutes or until the sauce is creamy and full of flavour. Serve immediately, garnished with extra rocket leaves.

FISH IN CRAZY WATER

PESCE ALL'ACQUA PAZZA

by Roberto Proto

This dish was developed hundreds of years ago when the sailors went to sea for months on end with just a few dried goods and not much else. The fish were caught and then garlic and a few tomatoes were added while it simmered in sea water! Delicious – although I wouldn't try the sea water these days. I'd stick to tap water unless you're feeling adventurous! Start with beautiful fresh fish and you have a dish that's hard to mess up.

SERVES 6

1.8 kg snapper, scaled and gutted (or use 6 × 250 g fillets)
200 g cherry tomatoes, cut in half
1 clove garlic, peeled and left whole
200 ml extra virgin olive oil
salt
pinch of finely chopped flat-leaf parsley

Preheat the oven to 150°C (fan-forced).

Combine the fish, tomato, garlic, oil, salt and 250 ml water in a flameproof baking dish and bake for 30–35 minutes. (If you are using fish fillets, halve the cooking time.)

Transfer the fish to a serving platter and remove the central bone and any other undesired ones. Remove the garlic clove from the baking dish, then put the dish on the stovetop over high heat and boil for 3 minutes or until the liquid has reduced slightly. Pour the sauce over the fish and garnish with a pinch of parsley. Dig in!

FROM LEFT,
MASSIMO, ROBERTO AND OTTAVIO

Roberto PROTO

ATRANI, RESTAURANT CO-OWNER AND CHEF

Another brilliant Amalfi Coast chef, Roberto loves to cook with flaming brandy, 1960s-style! It lights up his stove and he does it wonderfully: seafood, sides and sweets all see a little nip of brandy at some stage. As he often says when asked where he learnt to cook, 'My schooling was the Academy of the Streets!' Roberto followed all the usual steps of a great self-taught cook, graduating from bartending and washing dishes in his teens, to assisting an excellent chef, watching and learning every step of the way.

In the mid 1980s, Roberto and his brother Massimo bought a restaurant called A Paranza and employed a good chef. Roberto tucked himself away in the kitchen to assist the chef while Massimo worked the floor. Four years into this venture, the cook quit suddenly after a meltdown at the busiest time of the summer season and Roberto was left to fend for himself. His natural talents filled the void and the restaurant went from strength to strength. Their little eatery has no windows, no views of the undulating hills or the Mediterranean coast, no quaint piazza balcony – there's no drawcard but the great food. The restaurant is practically underground yet always full to the brim, even in winter. The locals know where to get a good meal and some of Roberto's recipes are so renowned in this area that I feel quite smug to have pried them from him – he's not one to hand them out freely.

Roberto believes in screamingly fresh seafood and that's just what you get. His fairytale town of Atrani has an annual day to celebrate the town's prize dish, sarchiapone – a huge marrow stuffed with vegies and meat – but Roberto, being totally dedicated to the sea, stuffs his giant marrow with vegies and seafood. It's a winner!

Today Roberto is the head honcho in his kitchen and need never again fear kitchen meltdowns – not only has his very capable second chef Ottavio been at his side for the past twelve years, but Roberto has truly become one of the Amalfi Coast's star chefs.

ROBERTO'S RECIPES

Tanina VANACORE

POSITANO, RESTAURANT OWNER AND CHEF

Tanina was always the 'hot cookie' of Positano: gorgeous-looking, fast as lightning and a huge talent in the kitchen. She was dynamic thirty years ago when I arrived in Positano and she still is today. Over the decades I've known her, she's run a great eatery and fabulous cooking schools, and always been somehow involved in food.

Tanina's mother was an excellent cook and worked for an aristocratic family in Naples, travelling two hours each day by train. From an early age, Tanina would often tag along and sit for hours in that Neapolitan kitchen watching her mother produce one delectable dish after another; she had no choice but to absorb the family talent. She played with bread dough, mixed leftover vegetable scraps with flour and water and basically made plenty of 'messy' food pies.

At a young age she married a gentle soul called Carlo Attanasio and produced two lively kids between restaurants and cooking schools. Tragically, Carlo passed away before turning fifty and Tanina's world was shattered. But Tanina took on the challenge of her new life and opened yet another classy restaurant, Next 2, with her children (who by then were young adults), showcasing her innovative style of cooking tapas-style food using very traditional Italian ingredients. The little restaurant in the heart of town was an instant success. Once it was up and running, in the capable care of her daughter Carmela, Tanina opened

a little boutique just down the road, selling elegant souvenirs and stylish local gifts. Carmela excels with her desserts and I could eat an entire meal of them.

Every so often Tanina reappears in the restaurant kitchen to thrill us all. Her favourite dish to prepare is the classic parmigiana di melanzane (eggplant parmigiana), learnt from her Mama many years ago, and her favourite dish to eat is pasta, provola, potatoes and basil, a delicious, classic poor-man's dish. Today, clever Tanina has reworked these unbeatable traditional flavours to create contemporary bliss, adding to the fine reputation of the super-chic Next 2.

The name of this dish comes from the French word 'surtout' (or 'soprattutto' in Italian), which means especially or above all. The reason for this is evident in the construction of this dish, with the rice sitting on top of the meatballs. Take my advice and eat like a pauper for at least a day before you try tackling this dish – it's the perfect meal for a rugby team with ravenous appetites!

SERVES 6

2 litres good-quality vegetable stock
2 tablespoons extra virgin olive oil
½ medium white onion, finely chopped
500 g carnaroli rice
salt
30 g butter
50 g parmesan, grated
fresh breadcrumbs made from stale bread (see page 30), for sprinkling
250 g fresh or frozen baby peas
100 g Neapolitan salami, cut into small dice
200 g smoked provola cheese, cut into small dice
basil leaves, to garnish

MEATBALLS

3 slices of stale bread
200 g minced veal
1 teaspoon salt
a few grinds of pepper
500 ml peanut oil

TOMATO SAUCE

100 ml extra virgin olive oil
2 white onions
1 kg canned Italian tomatoes

TRADITIONAL BAKED RICE DISH

SARTÙ DI RISO

by Tanina Vanacore

Bring the stock to the boil in a large saucepan. Reduce the heat and keep at a low simmer. Heat the oil in a large heavy-based saucepan over medium–low heat, add the onion and cook until lightly golden. Add the rice and stir for a minute or two until well coated in the oil mixture. Increase the heat to high. Add the hot stock, one ladle at a time, stirring until the liquid has been absorbed before adding the next one. Continue in this way for about 15 minutes or until the rice is cooked but al dente. Add a little salt (but not too much), then stir in the butter and parmesan and leave the risotto to cool.

To prepare the meatballs, dip the bread in water and then squeeze dry. Combine with the minced veal, salt and pepper, then form the mixture into walnut-sized balls. Heat the oil in a large heavy-based saucepan until very hot but not smoking. Add the meatballs (in batches if necessary – you don't want to overcrowd the pan) and cook for a few minutes until browned all over. Remove with a slotted spoon and drain on paper towels.

Preheat the oven to 180°C (fan-forced). Grease a 15–18 cm round or square baking dish (about 10 cm high) and sprinkle with breadcrumbs.

When the risotto has cooled, gently stir in the peas, salami and provola. Spoon half the risotto into the baking dish and gently press down with the back of a spoon. Make small dents in the surface of the rice and place a meatball into each one. Spoon over the remaining risotto to cover and gently press down again. Bake for 25 minutes or until the cheese has melted.

Meanwhile, to make the sauce, heat the oil in a medium heavy-based saucepan over medium–low heat, add the onion and cook until transparent. Add the tomatoes and cook for 30 minutes. Season to taste with salt.

When the rice bake is ready, loosen the sides carefully and turn out onto a large serving plate. Cut the sartu into portions and drizzle the sauce over the top. Finish with a garnish of basil leaves.

THIS ELABORATE DISH WAS ANOTHER FAVOURITE AMONG THE NEAPOLITAN ARISTOCRACY DURING THE 1700s. TECHNICALLY, THIS RECIPE SERVES SIX PEOPLE AS A PRIMO, BUT REALLY SHOULD BE DIVIDED AMONG FOUR OR FIVE PEOPLE SO THERE IS A GREATER SENSE OF ABUNDANCE. FOR THIS REASON IT IS MORE OFTEN EATEN AS A SECONDO.

THE FAMOUS SALSA NAPOLITANA (NEAPOLITAN TOMATO SAUCE) IS A STAPLE IN EVERY KITCHEN ON THE COAST. THE GENERAL RULE IS FOR EVERY 100 GRAMS OF TOMATOES, 10 MILLILITRES OF EXTRA VIRGIN OLIVE OIL IS REQUIRED – PLUS YOUR CHOICE OF ONION, GARLIC AND BASIL, NATURALLY!

SARDINES WITH BAKED POTATOES AND CHERRY TOMATOES

SARDINE con le PATATE I POMODORINI al FORNO

by Gianni Irace

This light, delicious dish is the ideal secondo after you've enjoyed a substantial primo. The primo is so loved in this part of Italy that by nature the secondo has become just that – a second dish, a delightful afterthought. These little fish served with a fresh-flavoured sauce are a perfect example. And Gianni makes them with such love.

SERVES 6

180 ml extra virgin olive oil
2–3 cloves garlic, chopped
1–2 long chillies, finely chopped
900 g dutch cream potatoes, peeled and very thinly sliced
1.5 kg fresh sardines, cleaned, scaled and gutted, bones removed
500 g cherry tomatoes, cut in half
3 tablespoons roughly chopped flat-leaf parsley
2 teaspoons salt
1 white onion, cut into rings
crusty bread, to serve

Preheat the oven to 180°C (fan-forced).

Pour the oil into a large baking dish, scatter with the garlic and half the chilli, then top with a layer of potato. Put a layer of sardines on top of the potato, then some of the tomatoes, some parsley and salt. Add a scattering of onion rings.

Continue to layer the remaining ingredients in this way, finishing with a final onion layer. Pour over 4 tablespoons of water and bake for 50–60 minutes or until the potato is tender. Serve with crusty bread.

THIS IS A CLASSIC ANCIENT PRAIANO RECIPE WHERE THE SARDINES GIVE FLAVOUR TO THE POTATOES AND THE POTATOES GIVE BODY TO THE SARDINES. A WONDERFUL MARRIAGE!

When I last visited Felice, it was 10 o'clock in the morning and she was already preparing lunch! These tasty little fish were all neatly lined up on her bench, ready to be dressed and heated, but I couldn't help wondering how she was going to reheat them at lunch time. 'No need,' she said, offering me a few to try. 'They are as delicious cold as they are hot!' I love these easy dishes that offer plenty of choices.

SERVES 6

1 tablespoon extra virgin olive oil
1 kg medium fresh sardines, cleaned, scaled and gutted,
    tail left on, patted dry
mint leaves and lemon, to garnish (optional)

DRESSING

125 ml extra virgin olive oil
juice of 1 lemon
250 ml white wine
2½ tablespoons white wine vinegar
1 clove garlic, finely chopped
15–20 mint leaves, torn

Preheat the oven to 180°C (fan-forced).

Grease a baking tray with the oil and heat in the oven for 10 minutes. Add the sardines in a single layer and bake on the bottom shelf of the oven for 10 minutes (adjust the cooking time up or down slightly if the sardines are very small or very large). Move the tray to the top of the oven and bake for a further 5 minutes.

Meanwhile, to make the dressing, mix the ingredients together in a small bowl with a spoon or fork.

Transfer the sardines to a flat serving dish and pour the dressing evenly over the top. Garnish with mint leaves and lemon if liked and serve hot, tepid or at room temperature.

ROASTED AND DRESSED FRESH SARDINES

SARDINE ARROSTITE E CONDITE

by Felice Fiore

DOLCI

AMALFI COAST LEMON DELICIOUS

DELIZIA AL LIMONE

by Erika Villani

Invented by the great Sorrentine pastry chef Carmine Marzuillo, this recipe has become so diffused in the various regions around Campania that everyone feels like it belongs to them. Sorrento is just a small hop away from the Amalfi Coast so we feel we have something to claim, particularly because we possess the famous protected Amalfi lemon 'lo sfusato' which enhances the flavours of this delightful dish with its sweet juices, seedless flesh and tasty peel.

SERVES 4

100 ml boiling water
50 g sugar
100 ml Limoncello
300 g prepared sponge cake (or homemade,
   if you happen to have some)

CUSTARD

4 egg yolks
150 g caster sugar
45 g plain flour, sifted
500 ml milk
peel of 1 lemon, in strips
200 ml pouring cream, whipped
100 ml Limoncello

Make a quick sugar syrup by combining the boiling water and sugar in a heatproof bowl. Stir until the sugar has dissolved, then set aside to cool. Mix 100 ml sugar syrup with 100 ml Limoncello.

To make the custard, place the egg yolks and sugar in an electric mixer (or use hand-held beaters) and beat until light and fluffy. Add the flour and mix well until smooth. Combine the milk and lemon peel in a small saucepan and bring to the boil. When the peel rises to the surface, turn off the heat and remove the peel. Slowly add the warm milk to the egg and sugar mixture, whisking constantly. Pass the mixture through a fine-meshed sieve to remove any lumps, then pour into a small saucepan and whisk over low heat until it reaches boiling point. Turn off the heat and stir well, then set aside to cool completely. Fold in the whipped cream and Limoncello.

Cut the sponge cake into pieces that will fit four small glass dishes, then briefly soak the sponge in the sugar syrup and Limoncello mixture.

Pour a layer of custard into the dishes (or scooped-out lemons, like we have in the photo), filling the dish to about one third. Top with a layer of soaked sponge, then finish with a second layer of custard. Refrigerate for 1 hour before serving.

LEMON ECLAIRS

BIGNÈ con CREMA al LIMONI

by Angela Giannullo

It is impossible to stop at one of these 'pop in the mouth' delights. The art is to keep the pastry light and neutral, allowing the famous Amalfi 'sfusato' lemon flavour to shine in the custard. Make sure your lemons have a sweet tang, rather than sour, and let the lemon zest have a good long soak in the milk overnight.

SERVES 8

1 teaspoon salt
200 g butter
400 g strong plain flour (such as Italian '00')
8 eggs
icing sugar, for dusting

LEMON CUSTARD

1.5 litres milk
grated zest of 2 lemons
10 egg yolks
300 g caster sugar
100 g strong plain flour (such as Italian '00'), sifted
100 g cornflour

To make the lemon custard, combine the milk and half the lemon zest in a bowl and leave to soak for at least 4 hours, preferably overnight.

Place the egg yolks and sugar in an electric mixer (or use hand-held beaters) and beat until light and fluffy. Add the flour and cornflour and beat until smooth. Transfer the mixture to a medium saucepan. Strain the milk and lemon, then gradually add the milk to the pan, stirring constantly over low heat until creamy and smooth. Allow to cool completely, then stir in the remaining lemon zest.

Preheat the oven to 200°C (fan-forced). Line a large baking tray with baking paper.

Pour 500 ml water into a large saucepan, add the salt and butter and gently bring to the boil over medium heat. When it starts to boil, reduce the heat to low and add the flour all at once. Stir vigorously with a wooden spoon for about 5 minutes until the mixture forms a large ball and separates from the side of the pan. Transfer the dough to a bowl and set aside to cool for about 10 minutes. Add the eggs, one at a time, and beat with a wooden spoon until combined.

Spoon the dough into a piping bag and squeeze out dollops the size of a walnut onto the prepared baking tray. Bake for 20 minutes or until puffed and golden. Remove and cool completely on a wire rack.

Spoon the lemon custard into a piping bag, then pipe a little into each eclair. Arrange the eclairs on a pretty serving plate and dust with icing sugar. You may also like to decorate the plate with lemon leaves.

ANGELA COOKS FOR AN EXCLUSIVE RENTAL PROPERTY CLOSE TO A BEACH IN POSITANO WHERE MY FRIENDS AND I WOULD LAZE AWAY THE LONG SUMMER DAYS. ONCE I HAD BEGGED ANGELA FOR THIS RECIPE SHE COULDN'T WAIT TO SHOW OFF HER ECLAIR TALENT! ONE DAY SHE APPEARED ON THE BEACH WITH A LARGE TRAY OF THESE LEMON DELICACIES. IN NO TIME AT ALL, MY SMALL GROUP OF TWO FRIENDS HAD SUDDENLY GROWN TO A DOZEN!

RICH CHOCOLATE AND ALMOND CAKE

TORTA CAPRESE

by Mena Vanacore

This cake is a classic in this area of Campania and you will find it on many menus. Unfortunately, it can be dry, heavy and indigestible unless served with buckets of ice-cream and cream. Mena's version, however, is thick, rich, moist and delicious, and needs no accompaniment (although a little scoop of vanilla ice-cream is traditional). Mena gave me her recipe many decades ago when she was just a teenager, already showing great prowess in the kitchen.

SERVES 10

200 g butter, softened
300 g caster sugar
7 eggs, separated
pinch of salt
400 g almonds with skin
1 teaspoon cocoa powder
200 g dark chocolate, shaved with a large knife
1 teaspoon baking powder
icing sugar, for dusting
vanilla ice-cream, to serve

Preheat the oven to 120°C (fan-forced) and line a 22 cm springform tin with well-greased baking paper.

Place the butter and sugar in an electric mixer (or use hand-held electric beaters) and beat until pale and fluffy. Add the egg yolks, one at a time, beating well between additions.

Whisk the egg whites and a pinch of salt until stiff peaks form.

Finely chop the almonds in a coffee grinder or similar. Combine with the cocoa and shaved chocolate.

Gradually add the almond and chocolate mixture to the creamy butter mixture, beating constantly. The dough will become quite firm. Gently fold in the egg whites with a spatula, and then fold in the baking powder.

Pour the batter into the prepared tin and bake for 20 minutes, then increase the heat to 180°C and bake for another 30 minutes. Turn off the oven and leave the cake to cool in the oven for 5 minutes with the door slightly open. Remove and cool in the tin for a few more minutes, then turn out onto a plate or cake stand and carefully remove the baking paper. Leave it upside down and dust with icing sugar (using a stencil pattern if you like). Serve with vanilla ice-cream.

NOTE *A delicious variation (strictly for the adults!) is to add 1½ tablespoons rum when folding in the egg white.*

ANGELA AND HUSBAND BENIAMINO

Angela GIANNULLO

FURORE, PRIVATE VILLA COOK

Many years ago I let an eleventh-century tower in Positano to a group of funny loud Australian friends. Angela had been cooking for the property owner (a real life princess!) for more than a decade, but my friends wanted to steal her, bring her back to Sydney and lock her in their kitchen forever. Her food is totally balanced; she barely uses a grain of salt and you'd never miss it.

Originally from the mountain-top town of Furore, Angela has been a permanent fixture in Positano for decades. Sweet and gentle, she is totally dedicated to her oven.

When Angela was a young girl, her family had a restaurant near her home town and this is where she started cooking. But life was not always easy during her early years and she often struggled to achieve success in the kitchen. Her grandmother instructed her to use lard rather than butter in her desserts and cakes, which was her favourite thing to cook, but Angela dreamed of cooking with butter. Her mother was a farmer and owned cows, so Angela would skim the top off the milk and shake it vigorously in a jar until she got the butter. Her enthusiasm and vigour did not always result in a perfect dish, and her mistakes would end up in the farm's pig pen so her mother wouldn't discover them.

Angela would like to spend more tranquil time cooking for her beloved husband Beniamino in their wonderful terraced house on the mountain top in Furore. Her motto in the kitchen is 'never ever give up – sooner or later you'll get it right'. And she's proved that, again and again.

Mena VANACORE

POSITANO, VILLA GUARDIAN AND HOUSEWIFE

I've known Mena since she was a baby paddling in the water on Laurito beach, where I lived for nearly twenty years. I watched her grow up and was always captivated by her fluorescent green eyes. One day, when Mena was about fourteen or fifteen, she brought her chocolate and almond cake down to the beach for the Da Adolfo staff to try. She was the sister of our boat boy Rocco, and we didn't want to hurt her feelings, so we tucked in. But Rocco, who knew what we were in for, watched us with laughter in his eyes. I've never to this day eaten a better chocolate and almond cake: moist and rich, it sent me into spins and I didn't give up until Mena gave me her recipe. I've been making this cake ever since, and am always showered with compliments.

Mena helped her mother and grandmother in the kitchen and watched, learnt and experimented from an early age. Rocco would bring home fish he'd caught at night and Mena would prepare it. She confesses that her first experience of baking one of Rocco's fish with potatoes was a nightmare of nerves and tension. She not only surprised her entire family but also herself – it was a triumph!

Mena's motto in the kitchen is 'Spices and herbs are what make a meal distinctive'. She's always on the hunt for the freshest basil, rosemary or oregano to add the final touch to make or break the end result.

Mena's daughter Ariana has followed in her footsteps, and Mena believes she too will be an excellent cook one day. Mena's ambition is to open a little eatery with Ariana. They plan to serve simple rustic meals and cook to their hearts' content. I believe they will – and win hundreds of hearts from all over the world with Mena's chocolate and almond cake!

AGATINA (LEFT) WITH HUSBAND MICHELE AND GRANDSON DIEGO

Agatina SEMPREVIVO

POSITANO, HOUSEWIFE AND DOUGHNUT STAR

Zeppole (Christmas doughnuts) are round and delicious, just like Agatina. She's the queen of the zeppole on the Amalfi Coast, having won numerous food competitions for her mouth-watering recipe and even demonstrated her doughnut prowess on national television. Agatina is such a jolly soul that you can't help but share her enthusiasm for this magical Christmas delight.

She claims that when she arrived in Positano more than forty years ago from her native island of Sicily she couldn't even boil an egg! After marrying a nice Amalfi Coast boy, she quickly understood that her role in life was to cook for her family. She taught herself at lightning speed and the zeppole were her first success. Her aim was to make them as soft as possible, and after a thousand attempts she finally achieved her dream, as six awards attest.

Agatina always dreamed of working in the top local patisserie. Alas, by the time her family was grown-up, she felt it was too late to move into a career. But her family and friends remain forever grateful, enjoying the fruits of her gifted and busy hands from her much-loved home kitchen.

Her talent doesn't end with the delectable doughnut: she also specialises in homemade pizzas and numerous tempting sweet treats. If it requires proving, rolling or dressing with honey, Agatina is the guru. Her little house is perched at the very top of Positano, right next to the local cemetery which enjoys the most spectacular views and blissful tranquillity. This is cooking heaven for Agatina.

AGATINA'S RECIPES

Many years ago, when families could not afford to buy sweets at Christmas, these delicate morsels were the perfect substitute. Agatina's grandmother and her friends would lock themselves away to prepare them, terrified that jealous prying noses would smell their delectability, bring bad luck and stop the doughnuts from rising!

Agatina frequently wins prizes for her zeppole and has even been on national television presenting them to the nation. She is the envy of the village and when you consider the number of prying noses the doughnuts attract, it's amazing they ever turn out!

MAKES 20-25

100 ml milk
300 g strong plain flour (such as Italian '00')
pinch of salt
25 g dried yeast
500 ml peanut oil
3 tablespoons honey
1 tablespoon sugar
25 ml Limoncello
grated zest of 1 lemon
1 teaspoon amarena cherries in syrup,
    drained and roughly chopped

Heat the milk and 260 ml water until warm. Sift the flour and salt into a large bowl and make a well in the centre. Place the yeast in the well, then slowly pour in the warm milk mixture, gradually incorporating all the ingredients with your fingers. When it is all combined, start to whip the dough with your hand, using it like a whisk and moving it towards you for 5 minutes to fold air into the dough. It should now be a thick, creamy consistency. This process could also be done in an electric mixer with a dough hook. Cover the dough with a plate or plastic film and leave in a warm place for at least 30 minutes until it has doubled in volume.

Heat the oil in a large heavy-based saucepan until very hot but not smoking. Take a dessertspoon of dough from the bottom of the bowl and, using a finger or teaspoon, drop into the hot oil. If it doesn't rise within 1 minute, the oil is not hot enough – you must let it heat properly otherwise the doughnuts will absorb too much oil. As soon as the doughnut rises to the top, flip it over using two spoons. Remove with a slotted spoon as soon as it is golden all over and drain on paper towels. Repeat with the remaining dough, but don't try to cook more than five at a time or the oil temperature will drop. When finished, place the well-drained zeppole on a serving dish.

Combine the honey and sugar in a small saucepan and bring to the boil. Stir in the Limoncello and lemon zest, then remove from the heat and pour over the doughnuts. Toss gently to coat and finish with a scattering of amarena cherries.

FRIED CHRISTMAS DOUGHNUTS

LE ZEPPOLE

by Agatina Semprevivo
(award-winning doughnut queen!)

THE ZEPPOLA LEGEND SPEAKS OF AN EGYPTIAN WOMAN MANY CENTURIES AGO WHO FELL ASLEEP WHILE SHE WAS KNEADING HER DOUGH TO MAKE UNLEAVENED BREAD. WHEN SHE AWOKE SHE SAW THAT THE DOUGH HAD DOUBLED IN VOLUME. NOT WANTING TO THROW IT AWAY SHE PICKED OFF SMALL CHUNKS OF DOUGH AND FRIED THEM UP. THEY WERE DELICIOUS! EVENTUALLY THE RECIPE ARRIVED ON THE AMALFI COAST. IT WAS THE CHRISTMAS PERIOD AND THE RECIPE WAS AMENDED TO INCLUDE MILK, YEAST AND HONEY. AND SO THE TRADITION OF CHRISTMAS ZEPPOLE WAS BORN.

LIGHT LEMON PLUM CAKE

This classic breakfast cake intrigued me from the first time I heard it called 'plum cake' in Italy – there's not a plum in sight! Valerio has coupled this iconic cake with the delicious flavour of Amalfi lemons. He usually makes mini cakes as shown in the photo, but has adapted the recipe here to make one large cake.

SERVES 8

400 g cake or dolci flour
2 tablespoons baking powder
good pinch of salt
2 tablespoons grated lemon zest
225 ml milk
150 g butter, melted and cooled
75 ml lemon juice
7 eggs
175 g caster sugar

Preheat the oven to 170°C (fan-forced). Grease and flour a 20 cm × 10 cm loaf tin.

Sift the flour and baking powder into a mixing bowl and stir through the salt and lemon zest.

In a separate bowl, combine the milk, melted butter and lemon juice.

Place the eggs and sugar in an electric mixer and beat for about 5 minutes until light and fluffy. You could also do this with hand-held electric beaters.

Fold alternate batches of the flour mixture and the milk mixture into the egg and sugar mix until a smooth batter is formed. Pour the batter into the prepared tin and bake for 50 minutes or until a skewer inserted into the centre comes out clean. Rest in the tin for a few minutes, then turn out onto a wire rack to cool, if liked, although it is delicious warm too.

Valerio serves this as a dessert with a splash of good Limoncello and a few strips of candied lemon peel (whipped cream is optional) OR as a breakfast cake, straight from the oven with a sprinkling of cinnamon or sugar. And if you don't have Valerio's stunning view of the Amalfi Coast, buy a poster and pretend. The cake will taste better!

LIGHT LEMON PLUM CAKE

by Valerio Buonocore

This is the naughtiest liqueur I have tasted since good ol' Limoncello hit the Amalfi Coast. High in the hilltop town of Ravello, I discovered its chocolate cousin. This indulgent after-dinner drop was developed by Valerio's mama Anna to delight her pensione guests. It can be sipped slowly to finish off the perfect meal, or it can be drizzled over creamy vanilla ice-cream. I have also enjoyed a slow glass at 11 o'clock in the morning – it was heaven, but don't go crazy. It DOES contain pure alcohol!

FILLS A 750 ML BOTTLE

1 cinnamon stick
1 star anise
125 ml pure alcohol (or a neutral-flavoured vodka)
400 g caster sugar
150 g cocoa powder
400 g milk

Soak the cinnamon stick and star anise in the alcohol for 20 days (if you are using ground spices, a pinch of each is all you need).

Combine the sugar and cocoa powder in a medium saucepan over low heat and add the milk, a little at a time, stirring constantly to make sure there are no lumps. Remove from the heat and allow to cool completely.

Strain the alcohol, discarding the spices. Add the cooled milk mixture and mix well, then pour into an elegant bottle with a good seal. Serve at room temperature so you can enjoy that wonderful chocolate flavour, and keep it well out of reach of children!

CHOCOLATE LIQUEUR

by Valerio Buonocore

SHORTBREAD CHESTNUT TART

by Valerio Buonocore

The woodlands surrounding Valerio's magnificent hilltop village of Ravello are busting at the seams with chestnuts during the month of October. Around this time, all the locals come from the neighbouring towns to celebrate the end of summer's chestnut season, and Valerio's baking takes on another dimension as chestnut-based ingredients rule. He is an expert after all!

SERVES 6-8
icing sugar, for dusting
vanilla ice-cream, to serve

SHORTBREAD PASTRY
500 g butter, softened
500 g caster sugar
7 egg yolks
5 eggs
1 kg cake or dolci flour, sifted

CHESTNUT FILLING
5 bay leaves
3 rosemary sprigs
200 g fresh chestnuts
150 g mixed berries (fresh or frozen)
75 ml red wine
200 g fresh ricotta
200 g caster sugar
75 g pine nuts, toasted

To make the shortbread pastry, place the butter and sugar in an electric mixer (or use hand-held electric beaters) and beat until pale and fluffy. Add the egg yolks, one at a time, then add the whole eggs, one at a time. Add the flour and mix for 1–2 minutes only. Wrap the dough in plastic film and rest in the fridge while you prepare the filling.

To make the filling, place the bay leaves and rosemary sprigs in a large saucepan with 2 litres water. Add the chestnuts and bring to the boil, then reduce the heat and simmer for 1½ hours or until the chestnuts become floury. Drain and leave until the chestnuts are cool enough to handle, then peel off the outer and inner shells. Press through a potato ricer or fine-meshed sieve with a spatula.

Combine the berries and wine in a small saucepan over high heat and boil for 5–6 minutes or until the wine has evaporated. Set aside to cool.

Preheat the oven to 170°C (fan-forced).

Place the chestnut puree, berries, ricotta, sugar and pine nuts in an electric mixer and blend until smooth.

Using a floured rolling pin, roll out the dough on a floured surface to a 5 mm thickness. Grease one large pie tin (about 32 cm) or 6–8 smaller tins (about 10 cm) and dust with flour. Line the tin or tins, reserving enough dough to create lids.

Spoon the filling into the pastry shell or shells, leaving a 5 mm gap at the top. Cover with the lid or lids, then prick the dough several times with a fork. Bake the large pie for 30 minutes and the smaller ones for about 15 minutes or until golden. Dust with icing sugar and serve warm with vanilla ice-cream.

The people of Maiori and Tramonti both claim this unusual recipe as their own. Either way, its roots go back to the Middle Ages when chocolate first arrived in Europe. Monks in this area would soak their eggplant in a delectable sweet herbal liqueur known today as Concierto, another native of Tramonti and also part of the original recipe. Some versions require the eggplant to be double, even triple-fried but Giuseppe's interpretation is lovely and simple.

SERVES 4

peel of 1 orange, cut into thin strips
peel of 1 lemon, cut into thin strips
420 g caster sugar
60 g strong plain flour (such as Italian '00')
pinch of salt
4 eggs
1 litre peanut or sunflower oil
2 eggplants (aubergines), peeled and cut into 1 cm thick rounds
300 g dark chocolate, broken into pieces
200 ml pouring cream
icing sugar, for dusting
mint leaves, cherries and edible flowers, to garnish (optional)

Blanche the orange and lemon peel in boiling water for 10 minutes. Meanwhile, dissolve 120 g sugar in 2 tablespoons water in a small saucepan over medium–low heat. Add the blanched peel to the sugar syrup.

Whisk together the flour, salt and eggs to make a batter.

Pour the oil into a large deep frying pan and heat to 190°C (a cube of bread dropped in the oil should brown in 10 seconds). Working in batches, quickly dip the eggplant rounds in the batter and drop into the oil until golden on both sides. Remove with a slotted spoon and drain in a colander.

Arrange the drained eggplant in a single layer on a large flat serving dish and sprinkle over the remaining sugar. Gently press the sugar into the eggplant with the back of a fork.

Place the chocolate and cream in a small saucepan over medium heat and stir until the chocolate has melted and the mixture is smooth.

Dip the eggplant rounds in the chocolate sauce, then layer with the caramelised citrus strips so that each serve has a stack of three. Finish with a final sprinkling of citrus, then dust with icing sugar and garnish with mint leaves, cherries and edible flowers (if liked).

CHOCOLATE EGGPLANT WITH CARAMELISED CITRUS FRUITS

MELANZANE AL CIOCCOLATO E AGRUMI CARAMELLATI

by Giuseppe Francese

CHOCOLATE AND RICOTTA PASTRY CAKE

by Carla Rispoli

I always think of Carla as belonging to one of the Great Pastry Chef Families of the coast, as her father and many aunties were regarded as talented pastry chefs, both locally and in America. They have more secrets in their scullery than the KGB have in Moscow! A few are so secret they are not even written down. For these delights, you will just have to visit her family restaurant in Positano, La Buca di Bacco. In the meantime, here is one recipe I managed to pry out of Carla. It's a bit of work, but worth every minute.

SERVES 8-10
3 tablespoons rum
3 tablespoons caster sugar
grated zest of 1 lemon
icing sugar, for dusting
chocolate-coated citrus peel and chocolate shapes,
   to decorate (optional)

SHORTCRUST PASTRY
230 g strong plain flour (such as Italian '00')
30 g caster sugar
pinch of salt
100 g butter, softened
4 tablespoons iced water (more if needed)

SPONGE CAKE
2 eggs
100 g caster sugar
80 g strong plain flour (such as Italian '00'), sifted
pinch of salt
½ teaspoon baking powder

RICOTTA FILLING
700 g fresh ricotta
300 g caster sugar (more if liked)
70 g dark chocolate, broken into small pieces (or use choc bits)
100 g mixed candied fruit, finely cut (optional)

To make the pastry, place the flour, sugar, salt and butter in a bowl and mix quickly and lightly with your fingertips until the mixture resembles coarse breadcrumbs. Add 1 tablespoon iced water at a time, mixing well between each addition with a fork, until the dough just starts to come together in clumps. Turn out the dough onto a well-floured marble or flat surface and gently press into a ball. Wrap in plastic film and rest in the fridge for a few hours. This can be done the day before, if liked.

Generously grease a 24 cm round cake tin. Roll out the dough very thinly on a floured surface then carefully line the tin and trim the edges. Prick the dough all over with a fork, then line with baking paper and fill with dried beans or chickpeas to stop it rising. Return to the fridge for at least 4 hours, preferably overnight. The longer the better.

Preheat the oven to 175°C (fan-forced). Bake the pastry for 20 minutes or until pale and dry, then remove the baking paper and beans or chickpeas and bake for another 15 minutes until golden. Remove and leave to cool completely.

To make the sponge cake, preheat the oven to 180°C (fan-forced). Grease a 24 cm round cake tin and lightly dust with flour. Place the eggs and sugar in an electric mixer and beat for about 3 minutes until light and fluffy (or use hand-held electric beaters). Gently fold in the flour, salt and baking powder with a large metal spoon. Pour the batter into the tin and bake for 15 minutes or until risen and lightly golden. Cool in the tin for a few minutes, then cool completely on a wire rack. Carefully cut a 2 cm-high horizontal layer from the cooled cake.

To make the filling, pass the ricotta through a ricer or fine-meshed sieve – you want it to be smooth and creamy. Transfer to a bowl and add the sugar, chocolate and candied fruit (if using). Mix together well.

Combine the rum, sugar, lemon zest and 125 ml water in a small saucepan and warm gently over low heat until the sugar has dissolved. Set aside to cool.

Pour the ricotta filling into cooled pastry case. Place the layer of sponge cake on top and sprinkle with the rum mixture. Do this carefully and slowly – it is far better to have liquid left over than to have a soggy cake!

Cover with a serving plate and turn out of the tin upside down so the pastry is on the top. Dust generously with icing sugar, then keep the cake cool in the fridge until you are ready to serve. If you like, decorate with chocolate-coated citrus peel and chocolate shapes.

NOTE *If you don't have time to make the sponge cake, simply replace it with a layer of Italian savoiardi biscuits (you'll need about 15). The results will still be delicious.*

CARLA'S KITCHEN TEAM

CARLA (RIGHT) WITH SISTER MARIANNA

Carla RISPOLI

POSITANO, OWNER OF THE ICONIC BUCA DI BACCO HOTEL-RESTAURANT

Carla Rispoli has a sweet and gentle disposition, just like her pastries. She's the granddaughter of the woman who started the first restaurant in Positano back in 1916. It was known back then as the Locanda Buca di Bacco (locanda 'inn', buca 'pit or cavity', Bacco 'Bacchus, the god of wine'). We can only imagine the result! Known today as the Buca di Bacco, or by the locals simply as La Buca, it's one of the finest restaurants in town.

I've always been fascinated by its big open kitchen window, through which passersby can easily see all that's being tossed, stirred, kneaded and chopped by a myriad of capable young chefs. To me, it seems a little like spying on something sacred!

Carla spent her early teens at the Buca behind the gelato counter. She was later promoted to the cash register and eventually found her way into the hotel side of the business, but she retained her grandmother's passion for food. Her aunts Maria and Anna were famous in Positano for their baking skills and spent a considerable amount of time in America over the years acquiring their secrets, using ingredients that aren't common in Italy, such as maple syrup and toffee. Today Carla and her sister Marianna (who is named after both aunts) carry these recipes around in their heads. Nothing is written down for fear it will be copied. Carla indulges in her favourite form of relaxation during the

winter months, when the family gets together for big cook-ups and those shared secrets become a delectable reality.

Today, everything that comes out of the Rispoli kitchen is truly amazing. The family has jealously guarded its recipes and kitchen secrets for nearly a century, so I feel utterly honoured that Carla has decided to share a few of them with us here. But for the iconic dishes (the cake called la splendida and the famous almond log), you'll just have to make the trip to Positano to try them yourself. Believe me, it's worth it!

MARTINE AND GIANNI

Gianni IRACE

PRAIANO, RESTAURANT OWNER

Gianni is the most hospitable restaurateur I've ever encountered. He and his Belgian wife Martine, both of whom studied at excellent hospitality schools, hooked up many moons ago while working in Switzerland. After years in the north, Gianni felt a cry for home and brought Martine back to the fairytale town of Praiano. He went off to work in a five-star hotel in nearby Positano while Martine tended the kids at home and whipped up wonderful homemade pastas and desserts. But they soon rented a little roadside trattoria, employed a few staff and opened the door of Ristorante La Brace in 1975. It did so well that they eventually bought the building, a great success story in this part of the world, where property is often impossible to purchase.

Gianni serves each and every guest with much love and attention. He's neither pushy nor aloof and his passion for food is palpable – he's a born restaurateur, and when he outlines the menu, you can almost taste the dishes. His standards are always high – no matter who's cooking on any given day, the food will be of top quality. Having said that, I believe he's employed only three chefs in more than thirty-five years: not a bad track record. But every now and then during the early years, Gianni would sometimes find himself in the kitchen when staff were off sick, tossing pans of pasta and simmering stews. This too could be part of his success: he tells me, 'If the owner can cook well, and staff do inevitably get sick, you never have a problem. Finding a waiter is a lot easier than finding a last-minute chef.' Gianni believes that part of his success in the restaurant business comes from understanding the food of his area, keeping it simple and serving dishes that have been around for many decades, sometimes centuries.

Martine is the queen of pastries and desserts, quietly delivering them to the restaurant each day, but she is like a mouse: I never laid eyes on her for my first fifteen years of living in Positano. Gianni lives for his restaurant and loves it. I can vouch for his dedication: no matter what time I drop by to say hello, he's always there. I'm sure he has a little bed tucked away somewhere behind the kitchen. Like many locals, his favourite pastime is fishing, but his dedication to La Brace gets in the way and he hardly ever finds the time to toss out a line these days. It's rare to find Gianni's restaurant doors closed at any time of the year. God bless you, Gianni! He's an institution in this neck of the woods and just as much a 'staple' as his pasta pomodoro.

CLASSIC EASTER CAKE

LA PASTIERA

by Martine and Gianni Irace

Baking this classic Neapolitan dessert is quite a lengthy process if you make everything from scratch (as given below), but if you don't have much time it's fine to use 300 ml top-quality ready-made custard and some really good ready-made sweet shortcrust pastry. The key here is the homemade filling. Pre-soaked wheat grain is readily available in good Italian delis, and makes the preparation all too easy, not to mention delicious!

SERVES 10

300 g soaked wheat grain, well rinsed
500 g fresh ricotta
5 egg yolks
peel of 1 orange, cut into thin strips
juice of 1 orange
200 g caster sugar
5 drops of vanilla essence
2–3 drops of orange blossom water
2 tablespoons chopped candied fruit (optional)
125 ml milk

PASTRY

375 g strong plain flour (such as Italian '00'), plus extra if needed
185 g butter, softened
185 g caster sugar
2 small eggs
3½ teaspoons baking powder

CUSTARD

2 egg yolks
1½ tablespoons strong plain flour (such as Italian '00')
2 tablespoons caster sugar
grated zest of 1 lemon
200 ml milk

To make the pastry, place all the ingredients in a bowl and mix together with your hands until well combined – if it gets too sticky add some more flour. Gently form into a ball and cover with plastic flim, then rest in the fridge overnight. Take the dough out of fridge 15 minutes before you are ready to start assembling the cake.

To make the custard, place the egg yolks, flour, sugar and lemon zest in a small saucepan. Whisk in a small amount of milk to make a smooth paste. Heat the remaining milk in a separate pan until it just reaches boiling point. Take off the heat immediately and whisk into the paste. Bring the mixture to the boil, stirring constantly, until the custard is thick and smooth. Set aside to cool.

Place the soaked grain, ricotta, egg yolks, orange peel, orange juice, sugar, vanilla, orange blossom water, candied fruit (if using) and custard in a large bowl and mix together with a wooden spoon. Add the milk and mix with your hands – this is important as you need to break up the grain and ricotta, and the best way is with lovely clean fingers! The mixture should be a similar consistency to a thick custard.

Preheat the oven to 180°C (fan-forced). Grease and flour a 32 cm round pie tin.

Using a floured rolling pin, roll out the dough on a floured surface to a thickness of 4–5 mm (you need enough to line the tin and cut out strips to decorate the top).

Line the prepared tin with the pastry, then pour in the ricotta filling to three-quarters fill the tin. Decorate the top with criss-crossed diagonal strips of pastry and bake for 45 minutes. To check that it's cooked, quickly put a wet finger under the tin – if it sizzles, it's ready! Let the cake cool before serving.

LA PASTIERA HAS A RICH HISTORY TO MATCH ITS FLAVOUR. KING FERDINANDO II'S WIFE, MARIA TERESA OF AUSTRIA, WAS KNOWN TO HER SOLDIERS AS 'THE QUEEN WHO NEVER SMILES'... UNTIL ONE DAY SHE WAS OFFERED A SLICE OF PASTIERA BY HER GLUTTONOUS HUSBAND, WHICH PRODUCED A WIDE SMILE. THE KING ANNOUNCED WITH GREAT SADNESS THAT HE'D HAVE TO WAIT FOR A FULL YEAR TO SEE HER SMILE AGAIN!

GRANDMA'S CUSTARD PIE

TORTA DELLA NONNA

by Consiglia Giudone

Every country in the world makes some sort of a custard pie and this version is a classic from this area. Consiglia offers her recipe as homage to grandmothers all over Italy – sacred figures in this part of the world. And as comfort food it is a blessing, especially when made with love by Grandma.

SERVES 8
5 egg yolks
110 g caster sugar
3½ tablespoons plain flour
500 ml milk
peel of 1 lemon
1 egg white, lightly beaten
55 g pine nuts or blanched almonds
icing sugar, for dusting

PASTRY
500 g strong plain flour (such as Italian '00')
250 g butter, softened
140 g icing sugar
1¼ teaspoon baking powder
1 egg
3 egg yolks
grated zest of 1 lemon

To make the pastry, place the flour and butter in a bowl and mix with hand-held electric beaters until the mixture resembles fine breadcrumbs. Add the icing sugar, baking powder, egg, egg yolks and lemon zest and gather gently into a ball. Don't overwork it or the dough will break up. Cover with plastic film and rest in the fridge for about an hour. It is a very soft dough so it must be well chilled and firm before you roll it out.

Place the egg yolks and sugar in an electric mixer (or use hand-held beaters) and beat until light and fluffy. Gradually add the flour and mix until smooth. Combine the milk and lemon peel in a medium saucepan and bring to the boil. When the peel rises to the surface, turn off the heat and remove the peel. Slowly add the egg and sugar mixture to the warm milk, whisking constantly over low heat until the custard is thick and smooth. Set aside to cool completely.

Preheat the oven to 150°C (fan-forced). Grease and lightly flour a 24 cm round cake or flan tin.

On a floured surface, roll out two-thirds of the dough to a thickness of 5–6 mm. Line the prepared tin with the dough and trim the edges, then pour in the custard. Roll out the remaining dough and place over the custard, pinching the edges together to seal. Brush the surface of the pie with egg white, then prick with a fork all over. Decorate with pine nuts or almonds and dust with icing sugar. Bake for 40–45 minutes or until lightly golden and cooked through. Serve warm.

WOODLAND SHORTBREAD BISCUITS

BISCOTTI DEL BOSCO

by Giuseppe Francese

A short time ago, I asked Giuseppe if 'cookies' were ever part of his repertoire in the kitchen. He threw his head back and laughed, saying how could they NOT be?! He makes them very casually in the midst of preparing complicated meat roasts, homemade pasta dishes and elaborate layered desserts. I think he enjoys them as a snack to calm the appetite between meals!

MAKES ABOUT 50

500 g strong plain flour (such as Italian '00')
200 g butter, softened and cut into 1 cm dice
200 g caster sugar
3 teaspoons baking power
1 teaspoon vanilla extract
3 egg yolks
grated zest of 1 lemon
grated zest of 1 orange
1 egg, lightly beaten
icing sugar, for dusting

Pile the flour into a mountain on a flat surface, make a well in the middle and add the butter, sugar, baking powder, vanilla and egg yolks. Mix well with your hands to form a dough, then add the lemon and orange zest and knead until combined. Form the dough into a ball, cover with plastic film and rest in the fridge for 30 minutes.

Preheat the oven to 190°C (fan-forced). Line two large baking trays with baking paper.

On a floured surface, roll out the dough to a thickness of about 3 mm. Using a biscuit cutter or cup, cut out whatever shapes you like (I like to keep them reasonably small). Place the shapes on the baking trays, leaving a little room for spreading, and brush with beaten egg. Bake for 10–12 minutes or until lightly coloured. Sprinkle with icing sugar and gobble them up while still warm, if possible (as Giuseppe and I did that day in Tramonti!).

Cannoli are much loved by Sicilians, but I find the pastry a little heavy and they tend to be loaded with candied fruit, which is not my favourite sweet. During a recent visit, Tanina blew me away when she and her gorgeous young daughter presented me with these bite-sized delights stuffed with ricotta, choc drops and pistachio nuts. Tanina and Carmela are masters in the art of dessert making and always do it with great enthusiasm and love.

MAKES ABOUT 20
icing sugar, for dusting (optional)

BISCUIT DOUGH
4 egg whites from small eggs
pinch of salt
80 g icing sugar, sifted
100 g butter, melted and cooled
100 g strong plain flour (such as Italian '00'), sifted

RICOTTA FILLING
400 g fresh ricotta, whipped
200 g icing sugar, sifted
4 tablespoons mini chocolate drops
60 g pistachios, toasted and roughly chopped
2 teaspoons finely grated orange zest

ORANGE SAUCE
3 oranges
4 tablespoons caster sugar
1½ tablespoons cornflour

To make the biscuit dough, whisk the egg whites with a pinch of salt until stiff peaks form. Gradually add the icing sugar, whisking constantly, then slowly add the cooled butter. Fold in the flour with a large metal spoon, then cover and rest in the fridge for 1 hour. During this time, the dough will thicken.

Preheat the oven to 180°C (fan-forced).

Place a sheet of baking paper on a flat surface. Take 2 teaspoons of the dough and spread it out with the back of the spoon to a 10 cm round. Transfer to a large baking tray, then continue with the remaining dough. Bake no more than five at a time for 4–5 minutes or until golden. As soon as they come out of the oven roll them up into a thick hollow cigar shape, using the end of a wooden spoon or cannoli tube to guide you. You need to work quickly while the biscuits are still warm and pliable, then set them aside to cool and harden.

To make the filling, place all the ingredients in a bowl and whisk until combined. Transfer to a piping bag and fill the biscuit tubes.

To make the sauce, peel the oranges (just the peel, not the pith) and cut the peel into very fine strips. Squeeze out the orange juice. Put the orange strips in a small saucepan with 250 ml cold water and bring to the boil over medium heat. Take off the heat as soon as it boils, then drain, reserving the peel. Repeat this process twice more.

Combine the sugar, orange peel and juice in a small saucepan over medium–low heat and simmer gently for 5 minutes or until the sugar has dissolved. Add two drops of tepid water to the cornflour and stir to remove any lumps. Take the orange mix off the heat and stir in the cornflour paste, mixing well. As it cools it will thicken.

When you are ready to serve, place two cannoli on each plate and drizzle over the orange sauce. Dust with icing sugar, if liked, and serve with pride!

NEAPOLITAN CREAM HORNS

CANNOLI NAPOLETANI

by Tanina Vanacore

THE FAMOUS AMALFI COAST RICOTTA AND PEAR PIES

TORTA DI RICOTTA E PERE

by Vera Milano

Recently, my talented design friend Giacomo and I enjoyed a sparkling seaside lunch at Vera's restaurant. We were bowled over by her little ricotta and pear biscuit sandwiches (not the usual cake slabs) and managed to pry the recipe from her. Giaco loves a baking challenge so we got straight to work that night – it was a little fiddly but well worth it. Ours were not as pretty as Vera's but they tasted outrageously good!

MAKES ABOUT 15

icing sugar, for dusting

BISCUIT DOUGH

500 g strong plain flour (such as Italian '00'), sifted
2½ teaspoons baking powder
200 g caster sugar
250 g butter, softened
1 tablespoon finely grated lemon zest
1 egg
2 egg yolks
3 drops of vanilla extract
20 g concentrated hazelnut paste (optional)

RICOTTA CREAM

400 g good-quality canned pears, syrup drained and reserved, pears cut into 1 cm dice
150 g sugar
½ teaspoon rum
½ cinnamon stick
6 gold-strength gelatine leaves, softened in water and squeezed out
500 g fresh ricotta, well drained of all liquid
175 g icing sugar
100 ml thickened cream, whipped to stiff peaks

To make the biscuit dough, pour the flour and baking powder onto a flat marble or wooden surface and make a well in the middle. Add the remaining ingredients and gently bring together to form a ball of dough. Knead well for about 5 minutes until smooth, then leave to rest for at least 5 minutes.

Preheat the oven to 175°C (fan-forced). Grease several large baking trays.

On a well-floured surface, roll out the dough to a 3 mm thickness. Using a 9 cm biscuit cutter or glass, cut out an even number of rounds (about 30). Place the biscuits on the trays and bake for 16 minutes or until golden (you may need to do this in batches). Cool on the trays for a few minutes then transfer to wire racks to harden and cool completely. These biscuits don't like hot, humid weather and tend to go soggy. To avoid this, store the cooled biscuits in the fridge while you continue with the recipe.

To make the ricotta cream, place the pear syrup, sugar, rum and cinnamon stick in a small saucepan and heat gently until lightly caramelised. Add the diced pear and cook until all the syrup has been absorbed. Remove the cinnamon stick.

Place the softened gelatine leaves and 1 tablespoon water in a small saucepan over low heat until melted. Cool. Beat the the ricotta and icing sugar in a bowl until smooth and creamy. Blend a small amount of the ricotta mix into the gelatine, then add the gelatine to the the ricotta mix and stir until smooth. Stir in the diced pear, then gently fold in the whipped cream with a large metal spoon. Cover and refrigerate for at least an hour so the mixture firms up.

Spoon the ricotta cream onto half the biscuits – you want the cream to sit about 2.5 cm high. Cover with the remaining biscuits and neaten the edges of the cream with a flat-bladed knife. Cover and refrigerate for at least 8 hours.

Just before serving, dust the pies generously with icing sugar. If you are having a celebration, cut out the initials of the person's name on paper and place on each pie before sprinkling with icing sugar. They will be chuffed!

DE RISO PATISSERIE IN MINORI IS FAMOUS FOR THIS RECIPE, WHICH APPEARED ON THE AMALPI COASTLINE 50-ODD YEARS AGO.
IN THE EARLY DAYS, WE WOULD HAVE TO DRIVE FOR 2 HOURS TO PICK ONE UP, BUT TODAY EVERY HOUSEHOLD, RESTAURANT, BAR, PATISSERIE AND TRATTORIA HAS ITS OWN VERSION.

DOLCI

BASIL GELATO

GELATO AL BASILICO

by Giuseppe Francese

I'm not quite sure what makes the basil leaf so exquisite on the Amalfi Coast, but I suspect it has something to do with the sun, the sea and the warm summer breezes. It grew in my garden like weeds! Basil is one of the most widely used herbs in this area, often served with fish and in salads, vegetables and stews, and more recently in Basiliconcello (the basil form of Limoncello)! But Giuseppe's basil gelato was a real revelation – sweet, delicate and utterly divine. It is the Italian flag or caprese salad (mozzarella, tomato and basil) of the dessert world!

SERVES 4

150 g caster sugar
25 g baby basil leaves, ground in a mortar and pestle
2 egg yolks
300 ml pouring cream
200 ml milk
pinch of salt
basil leaves, extra, to garnish
icing sugar, for dusting

TOMATO MARMALADE

200 g cherry tomatoes, cut in half, seeds removed
100 g sugar

If you don't have an ice-cream maker, put a 1-litre steel container in the fridge for at least 2 hours before you start. Place the caster sugar, ground basil, egg yolks, cream, milk and salt in an electric mixer and beat until pale green and creamy. (You could also do this with hand-held electric beaters).

If you have an ice-cream maker, pour the mixture into the machine and churn for about 20 minutes. Store in the freezer until you are ready to serve (it will probably need to firm up a bit).

If you do not have an ice-cream maker, pour the mixture into the chilled steel container, being careful to not fill it to the top, then place in the freezer for 1 hour. Take it out and mix vigorously, then return it to the freezer for another hour and mix again. Pour it into individual moulds or leave it in one container, then freeze for about 4 hours to do the final set.

To make the tomato marmalade, drop the tomatoes into boiling water for 1–1½ minutes, then remove and peel away the skin. Blend the tomatoes, then place in a small frying pan with the sugar and 100 ml water. Cook over medium heat, stirring constantly, until caramelised. Keep a close eye on this: if the mixture starts to crystallise, add more water and reduce down again.

Turn the gelato out of the moulds or scoop it out with an ice-cream scoop and serve with the tomato marmalade, fresh basil leaves and a sprinkling of icing sugar. If you have any caramelised fruit to hand (see, for example, the recipe on page 219), this also makes a lovely garnish.

I have always been partial to traditional tiramisu, but when I came to live on the Amalfi Coast, I quickly learnt there is so much more to this stunning dessert than I'd originally thought. It can be soaked in Limoncello, packed with Nutella, or layered with fine toffee – but for my money, Daniele's wild berry version wins hands down. If you love your coffee tiramisu as a winter dessert, this will break your heart in summer!

SERVES 8

5 eggs, separated
250 g caster sugar
500 g mascarpone
500 g mixed fresh or frozen berries
500 g Italian savoiardi biscuits

Place the egg yolks and sugar in an electric mixer and beat for 5 minutes until light and fluffy. You could also do this with hand-held electric beaters. Fold in the mascarpone.

Beat the egg whites in a separate bowl with clean beaters until stiff peaks form. Gently fold the egg white into the mascarpone mixture with a large metal spoon.

Blend 200 g of the berries with 300 ml of water until smooth, then pour into a shallow bowl.

Working quickly, dip the savoiardi biscuits into the berry mixture, one at a time. Arrange half the biscuits in a single layer in the base of a large serving dish. Spoon over half the mascarpone mix, then sprinkle with 100 g berries. Repeat with another layer of biscuits and mascarpone mix, then scatter over the remaining berries. Put the tiramisu in the fridge for at least 12 hours before serving.

NOTES *Start this gorgeous thing the day before you want to eat it, or at least early in the morning to serve that night. It really needs 12 hours in the fridge.*

Daniele's recipe is alcohol free (great for the kiddies) but can easily be modified for the adults with a splash of rum or vodka added to the berry puree.

BERRY TIRAMISU

TIRAMISÙ CON FRUTTI DI BOSCO

by Daniele Bella

CONTRIBUTING COOKS AND CHEFS

SOME FAVOURITE EATERIES

THE FOLLOWING RESTAURANTS AND BARS ARE FAVOURITES I HAVE EITHER RECENTLY DISCOVERED OR KNOWN ABOUT FOR MANY YEARS. THE MAJORITY ARE CHEF-OWNED AND THE FEW THAT AREN'T HAVE ALWAYS KEPT THEIR STANDARDS HIGH — REGARDLESS OF WHO IS COOKING. THE FOOD IS SUPERB!

POSITANO

NEXT 2
Viale Pasitea 242, Positano
Tel +089 8123516
www.next2.it

Talented Tanina is the founder of this jewel of a restaurant, and her clever daughter Carmela (the dessert queen) and talented boyfriend Renzo add to the amazing team in this chic eatery. Everything on the menu is mouthwatering. This is the place to come when you want to treat yourself to something special.

RESTAURANT IL RITROVO
Via Montepertuso 77, Positano
Tel +089 812005
www.ilritrovo.com

Come here for lunch on a hot summer's day, well away from the maddening beach crowd. It is cool, relaxing and a great way to eat your day away. Salvatore, the clever chef and owner, will appear with a fantastic antipasto spread, delicious cuts of meat and fabulous primi. The hanging tomatoes are the best!

DONNA ROSA
Via Montepertuso 97/99, Positano
Tel +089 811806
www.drpositano.com

This little hilltop family-run business produces five-star dining. Erika runs the kitchen with her mama and mentor Raffaela. They offer the best homemade pastas, delicious baked fish (the baked cod with peas and vongole is my favourite!) and delicately prepared desserts, all of which will tantalise your palate.

LA TAVERNA DEL LEONE
Via Laurito 43, Positano
Tel +089 875474
www.latavernadelleone.com

I just can't go past Fortunata's amazing homemade pastas – just looking at them makes me all warm inside – and the bread on the table comes directly from the restaurant's pizza oven. Everything you eat here is delicious, from classic minestrone to melted chocolate dessert, and everything in between!

BUCA DI BACCO
Via Rampa Teglia 4, Positano
Tel +089 875699
www.bucadibacco.it

This is the type of restaurant you can enjoy alone or with a crowd of friends. It is a total food experience with great service. They do the lightest of light fried seafood and if the hazelnut log is on the dessert trolley, book your portions as soon as you get there! There is also a small terrace overlooking the main beach – fabulous for a quiet sunset drink or a romantic dinner for two.

RISTORANTE LA CAMBUSA
Piazza A Vespucci 24, Positano
Tel +089 812051
www.lacambusapositano.com

Baldo and Danielle have always had great style, as do their clientele! Said to offer the best zuppa di pesce (fish soup) in town, they also offer a myriad of other tempting delights from the sea. Their classic spaghetti con le vongole (clam pasta) is an absolute winner – definitely not one not to miss!

RISTORANTE LE TRE SORELLE
Via del Brigantino 27–31, Positano
Tel +089 875452

If you have a large group and want a great fun dinner, this is the place for you. The owner Luigi looks after his clients wonderfully, and the waiters are so fast it's almost like they're wearing skates! Everything on the menu is prepared with great love and detail. Oh and this is THE hot spot for people-perving on the beach!

CHEZ BLACK
Via del Brigantino 27–31, Positano
Tel +089 875036
www.chezblack.it

Black is an institution in Positano – the owner himself and the restaurant. Whenever I go there I can't resist the sea urchin pasta dish – I just love theatrical way it is presented in a giant sea urchin. Crazy, but delicious!

LE TERRAZZE DELL'INCANTO (dinner only)
Via Grotte dell'Incanto 51, Positano
Tel +089 875874
www.leterrazzerestaurant.it

This is not a place to eat on your own as the romantic atmosphere would kill you! Candle-lit, pristine white, right on the water's edge and tucked into a quiet corner of the main beach, this is a romantic haven for fine diners. The waiters are gorgeous and the food is delicious!

BAR BRUNO RISTORANTE
Via Cristoforo Colombo 157, Positano
Tel +089 875392

Apart from the amazing view of Positano's main beach, I adore this place for its crazy set-up and delicious food. The waiters dart between cars and buses coming up the little hill to get from your table to Mario in the kitchen. Don't go past the pasta with rock fish – this to me is Mario's finest dish. Great prices too.

IL GROTTINO AZZURRO

Via Guglielmo Marconi 158, Positano
Tel +089 875466

Concetta (the owner) will take your order, her sons will serve you, and husband Raffa keeps an eye on what is cooking. This is by far one of my favourite trats in town: the baked pezzogna fish with baked sliced potato is fabulous, as are their homemade pastas. Check out the daily specials – they are always simple and delicious. Look out especially for pasta with beans or chickpeas.

C'ERA UNA VOLTA

Via Guglielmo Marconi 127, Positano
Tel +089 811930
www.ristoranteceraunavolta-
positano.com

Teresa and her team do not have the glamorous surroundings of the main beach, but she offers a charming view (much like herself!). The gnocchi dishes are authentic and hard to resist, as are the pizzas and local grilled fish. This is probably the best value little trat in town!

DA ADOLFO

Via Laurito 40, Positano
Tel +089 875022
www.daadolfo.com

It is tough for me to be objective about this little 'paradise', as Adolfo used to call it. For a joyful day by the sea with great food and fun, this is your spot. You can't go past their mozzarella on lemon leaves (invented by Adolfo and now adopted all over the coast!) OR a simple grilled fish with delicious mint dressing. This is a beachside institution on the coast and not to be missed, whether you are a party of two or ten!

BAGNI D'ARIENZO

Via Arienzo 16, Positano
Tel +089 812002
www.bagnidarienzo.com

The beach beds are blissful on a summer's day, and Ada's delicious food is the cherry on the cake. I could drown in her giant ravioli with provola, tomato and basil but when I'm having a skinny day, I go for her amazing little grilled fresh anchovies and a rocket and tomato salad. Simple but so delicious, and if Ada's husband Peppe is not too busy, he will dress the salad for you!

FORNILLO BEACH

PUPETTO BEACH BAR

Tel +089 875087
www.hotelpupetto.it/beach

GRASSI BEACH BAR

Tel +089 811620
www.grassibeachbar.com

DA FERDINANDO BEACH BAR

Tel +089 875365

These beachside restaurants are all about friends and family. There are plenty of locals down here to grab some rays, have a swim, play a hand of cards or eat a simple, delicious salad or giant panino. Sunset is quite early on this beach but in the very hot summer months, this can be a great relief – you can then stay on for a twilight apperativo!

LA SCOGLIERA BEACH ESTABLISHMENT - BEACH BAR

Spiaggia Grande, main beach, Positano
Tel +089 811822

This is the beach I go to when I want to hide, eat a fabulous tuna, rocket and tomato salad, drink a good coffee, swim in the clear water and not talk to a soul. A place to recharge my batteries. No kids, no loud music, no yelling boat boys. And I don't even have to move off my beach bed as the staff will serve me everything I need right there by the sea.

LA CONCA DEL SOGNO

Via San Marciano 9, Nerano
Tel +081 8081036
www.concadelsogno.it

Anna runs this beachside restaurant like a Swiss clock. ALL the antipasti are perfect, as are the pasta and fish dishes. This is not a cheap day out, but once you see the work that goes into preparing and serving this mind-blowing food, you will want to give Anna all your money! Order the 'big bunny' (Anna's pesce all'acqua pazza) in advance – you won't regret it.

RISTORANTE IL CANTUCCIO

Marina del Cantone, Nerano
Tel +081 8081288
www.ristorantecantuccio.com

The gorgeous and sultry Giovanna will be there to greet you as you get off the boat in Nerano, and before your wet swimmers hit the chair in her delightful restaurant, she will have a spread of delicious antipasti in front of you. She serves jugs of crisp white wine with hunks of 'percoca' local peaches – a great summer lunch at sea!

PRAIANO

RISTORANTE LA BRACE

Via Capriglione, Praiano
Tel +089 874226
www.labracepraiano.com

To me, this restaurant is home. I don't go for the decor or the view: the food is consistently good and has been for over 25 years. Gianni runs an excellent kitchen and every meal is exquisite, finished off perfectly with one of his wife Martine's famous pies! This is one of the few restaurants on the coast that is open all year round but please book: it is very well known among locals and travellers and you don't want to be disappointed.

RISTORANTE IL PIRATA

Via Terramare, Praiano
Tel +089 874377
www.ristoranteilpirata.net

This is my favourite seaside restaurant in Praiano, run by Vera, Rhino and their parents. If you are sleepy after eating at the water's edge with your feet practically dangling in the sea, just ask for a sun bed and brolly – they have a large flat rock under the eating terrace I call the 'snoozing station'! Quite simply, this place is paradise: daytime dining is idyllic, and an evening meal is romance on fire!

BAR MARE PETIT RISTORANTE

Via Marina di Praia 9, Praiano
Tel +089 874706

A great atmospheric spot for a late-night snack after a concert or just come to have a drink and chill out. By night, the charming owner Salvatore creates a wonderful ambience, playing terrific music which attracts a fun and local crowd; by day it's a great family spot. And all the while, his mama Clelia and her crew cook up a storm in the 'petit' kitchen!

FURORE

RISTORANTE AL MONAZENO
Via Anna Magnani, Furore
Mobile +39 3490772544
www.monazeno-fiordo-furore.com

Tucked away inside an enchanting 'fjord' right on the sea you will find Luigi's little restaurant, AND his delightful English! A must-try is his pasta with swordfish, rocket and cherry tomatoes. A great place for a quiet dinner for two or a fun lunch for ten, with good prices.

IL BACCO RESTAURANT
Hotel Ristorante Bacco,
Via G B Lama 9, Furore
Tel +089 830360
www.baccofurore.it

I love this place for the local produce – they serve wonderful hard and soft cheeses with local honey or jams at the end of the meal, and offer great wines from the owner's sister-in-law over the road. If you are looking for a traditional dish, just ask head chef (and the owner's wife) Ermina as she may just have something off the menu hidden in her pantry!

CONCA DEI MARINI

RISTORANTE LA TONNARELLA
Via Marina di Praia 1, Conca dei Marini
Tel +089 831939
www.ristorantelatonnarella.com

This is the best seaside restaurant in Conca. Arrive by boat or walk down the staircase from the main road. Enjoy excellent seafood in delightful surroundings on a tiny beach with a tiny ancient chapel that resembles a mini movie set! A lovely day out.

POLISPORTIVA RESTAURANT (now called Le Bontà del Capo and also a sports centre!)
Via I Maggio 14, Conca dei Marini
Tel +089 831515
www.amalficoast-restaurant.com

Il Capo is the gentleman who makes the ice-creams in this place, and he is also the owner! And what a treat those ice-creams are, not to mention the spaghetti with flying squid. In fact, everything is good in this newly renovated restaurant, and the view will take your breath away!

AMALFI

RISTORANTE BAR DA TERESA
Spiaggia Santa Croce, Amalfi
Tel +089 831237
www.dateresa.it

If you can, hire a boat, grab a big crowd of friends and have a fabulous day on the sea, with this as your fun lunch stop. This is the place to relax and enjoy one fabulous antipasto after another – they are so good I doubt you'll make it to dessert.

ATRANI

RISTORANTE A' PARANZA
Via Dragone, Atrani
Tel +089 871840
www.ristoranteparanza.com

This is one of the few Amalfi restaurants that does not hang over a beach, cliff, seaside or piazza! Nestled in a white-washed alleyway, A' Paranza has other fish to fry! Brothers Massimo and Roberto Proto (no relation to the Torre Normanna Protos in Maiori) will delight you with their love of all things hauled from the sea (the creamy seafood risotto is a must). It is essential to book as the 'Italians' staked their claim to this little gem many years ago and will not hand it over easily!

RAVELLO

CUMPA' COSIMO RESTAURANT
Via Roma 46, Ravello
Tel +089 857156

I love this place because of 'bossy' Netta, the owner, and the fact that so many Amalfi Coast taxi drivers sit up the back eating with Netta's husband while waiting for their ride to finish a tour of Ravello. Netta's food is wholesome and hearty (those drivers really need to keep up their strength!). There are no five-star views but it's just off the main piazza so it's a good place to stop for a quick lunch while taking in the sights in Ravello.

SCALA

RISTORANTE SAN GIOVANNI
Via S. Maria, Pontone, Scala
Tel +089 872582
www.ristorantesangiovanni.com

The restaurant has homemade or home-grown everything: the salami and gnocchi are a standout, and I'm sure they would make their own fish if they could! Don't let the slightly formal dining room scare you away – this is typical of the area. The terrace overhanging the coast is a marvel, with the Mediterranean stretching out beyond! Pure bliss.

L'ANTICO BORGO
Via Noce 4, Scala
Tel +089 871469
www.lanticoborgo.it

The pasta trios at this friendly restaurant will give you walking legs to get you back down to the seaside! Three succulent and different flavours wrapped around delicious pasta made on the premises. The pizzas are made with wholegrain flour and are hard to resist as you enjoy the stunning view! A glass or two of light local wine will keep you happy on your trek home.

MINORI

OSTERIA IL PONTILE
Via San Giovanni a Mare 25, Minori
Tel +089 877110
www.osteriailpontile.it

Previously owned by the Proto Brothers who now run the Torre Normanna in Maiori, this roadside trattoria has offered great-quality food and happy service for decades! Every morsel is worth the little extra you pay. Try the whole fish, or their sensational homemade pasta.

MAIORI

TORRE NORMANNA
**Via Diego Taiani 4, Maiori
Tel +089 877100
www.torrenormanna.net**

For a sparkling summer lunch, a romantic candle-lit dinner or a full-blown wedding reception, this place is a must-try. The Proto brothers are the best at what they do – they cook, serve, pamper and are true traditionalists. The simple dishes are my favourites (their spaghetti con aglio e olio is sensational) but Massimo and Gigi's kitchen prowess can achieve anything.

TRAMONTI

CUCINA ANTICHI SAPORI
**Via Chiunzi 72, Tramonti
Tel +089 876491
www.cucinaantichisapori.it**

Giuseppe's passion for food shows on every plate. His gnocchi di castagna is heavenly and, being a mountain boy, he knows how to cook meat properly. So if you are a struggling non-fish eater, this spot will be your salvation – his pork and lamb dishes are particularly delicious.

OSTERIA REALE
**Via Cardamone 75 – Fraz. Gete, Tramonti
Tel +089 856144
www.osteriareale.it**

Luigi Reale is the jolly face behind this exceptional countryside eatery. With his own wine cellars full of quality vino and the panorama overlooking his magnificent vineyards, this lunch experience should give you great joy. Try his parmigiana di melanzane e alici – it is heaven.

TENUTA SAN FRANCESCO WINERY
**Via Solficiano 18, Tramonti
Tel +089 876748
www.vinitenutasanfrancesco.it**

This is a wine taster's delight with the best, most wholesome country food to boot! Everything is prepared with great love and tenderness – and you don't have to order: they just bring out the food and tell you which wine to drink with each scrumptious dish.

CETARA

RISTORANTE ACQUA PAZZA
**Corso Garibaldi 38, Cetara
Tel +089 261606
www.acquapazza.it**

This is fine dining at its best, with extraordinarily fresh produce (they have their own fishermen!). Instead of salt at each table there is a precious bottle of fresh anchovy syrup. A must-try. Mortgage the house and order the lobster pasta – I promise it is worth every mouthful.

RISTORANTE PIZZERIA AL CONVENTO
**Piazza San Francesco 16, Cetara
Tel +089 261039
www.alconvento.net**

Here you can enjoy delicious home-style cooking while gazing up at some of the most wonderful wall mosaics from the 1500s, which were part of the cloisters of the church of S. Francesco. Just wonderful – well priced and great anchovy pizza!

VIETRI SUL MARE

RISTORANTE 34 'DA LUCIA'
**Via Scialli 48, Vietri sul Mare
Tel +089 761822
www.risto34dalucia.altervista.org**

Known as a great local cook, Lucia decided to turn herself into a business. Brilliant! Set in a quirky creative piazza, the restaurant is like home, with Lucia tossing the pots and pans. Try her stuffed zucchini – they are absolutely delicious, and really good value too.

A NOTE ABOUT PRICES

I've noticed that the simplicity and generosity of the Amalfi Coast lifestyle can give visitors the impression that prices will be low. I can only say that the quality of everything has improved immensely over the last couple of decades. Remember that the entire coastline is only 40 kilometres, and seafood is expensive all over the world. The locals take great pride in their food, and just because a meal is served on a rickety old chair on a pebbled beach does not mean it will cost 20 euro. When you pay a little more for something special (including your magnificent surroundings), rest assured there will be a little delight around the corner that will surprise you. I am very aware of rents and wages in this country and marvel that the Italians, especially the seasonal workers of the Amalfi Coast, manage to make ends meet. So please pay with a smile!

This list is not exhaustive. Obviously I have not eaten at every restaurant on the Amalfi Coast, and I don't have space to mention all the wonderful hotel restaurants that accept outside bookings – and there are plenty! And don't even get me started on beach bars! I can only hope you will discover many wonderful Amalfi eateries of your own. I'd love to hear about them, so please feel free to email me.

For a first-class 'food safari' along the Amalfi Coast, please contact me at book@amandatabberer.com. Available May/June and September/October.

ITALIAN
FOOD AND WINE IMPORTERS IN AUSTRALIA

HERE ARE NINE OF AUSTRALIA'S BEST ITALIAN FOOD AND WINE IMPORTERS. THEY WILL HAPPILY GIVE YOU DETAILS REGARDING YOUR CLOSEST RETAIL OUTLETS ALL OVER AUSTRALIA WHO CAN SUPPLY YOU WITH ARTISAN PASTAS AND TOP-QUALITY CANNED TOMATOES AND EXTRA VIRGIN OLIVE OILS, PLUS MANY OTHER GOODS YOU MAY NEED TO PREPARE THE AUTHENTIC AMALFI COAST DISHES INCLUDED IN THIS BOOK. BUON APPETITO!

COSTA FINE FOOD
costafinefood.com.au
Tel 02 9748 8201

CASA ITALIA GOURMET FOOD & WINES
casaitalia.com.au
Tel 1300 909 400

BASILE IMPORTS
basile.com.au
Tel 1800 635 268

LEO'S IMPORTS
leosimports.com.au
Tel 03 9359 0658

ZANCHI IMPORTS
zanchiimports.com
Tel 03 9460 1300

PACCHINI & SONS
pacchiniandsons.com.au
Tel 02 9725 5000

NAPOLI FOOD SUPPLIES
napolifoodsupplies.com.au
Tel 02 9519 4411

ITALIAN FOOD
italianfood.com.au
Tel 02 9748 7569

QUALITY CENTRE
qualitycentre.com.au
Tel 02 9748 6633

GRAZIE MILLE A...

GRAZIE MILLE TO ALL THE WONDERFUL CHEFS AND COOKS OF THE AMALFI COAST!
I AM ETERNALLY GRATEFUL TO YOU ALL FOR THE TIME AND KNOWLEDGE YOU SO GENEROUSLY
SHARED WITH ME AND WHICH, IN TURN, I AM PASSING ON TO MY HAPPY READERS.

A HUG TO MY MUM MAGGIE FOR BEING THE BEST SOUNDING-BOARD IN THE WORLD.
SHE MUST HAVE READ EVERY PAGE OF THIS BOOK A HUNDRED TIMES BUT SO GRACIOUSLY
GAVE HER TIME, EXPERT ADVICE AND ENCOURAGEMENT TO KEEP MY VOICE AND
ENFORCE EVERYTHING ELSE SHE HAS TAUGHT ME OVER THE YEARS!

'GRAZIE' TO MARCO BELLA, MY SON, FOR PATIENTLY CORRECTING MY SOMETIMES 'SHAKY'
ITALIAN GRAMMAR, BEING THERE TO LISTEN WHEN I HAD MY DOUBTS, AND ALWAYS
OFFERING SOUND ADVICE.

THANK YOU TO MY DARLING SISTER BROOKIE AND MY VERY ITALIAN BROTHER NICO
FOR ALWAYS BEING THERE.

A BIG SQUEEZE TO DANIELE BELLA FOR HIS PATIENCE AND DEDICATION TO HIS
PROFESSION AS A GREAT CHEF, AND FOR SO GENEROUSLY SHARING HIS TALENTS
AND SKILLS WITH ME, INCLUDING HIS INSTINCTIVE NEAPOLITAN 'SPELL CHECKS'!

TO ALL THE AMALFI COAST LOCALS WHO GUIDED ME TOWARDS THE BEST 'FOODIE TRAILS'
IN THIS REGION: I AM SO GRATEFUL AND CAN'T WAIT FOR OUR NEXT MEAL TOGETHER!

EVI OETOMO, YOU ARE A GRAPHIC TREASURE. I BLESS YOUR DRIVE, ENTHUSIASM AND
TALENT, NOT TO MENTION YOUR PATIENCE WITH ALL THE FINER DETAILS OF THIS
BOOK TO BRING OUT THE VERY BEST IN MY BELOVED AMALFI COAST RECIPES.

MY DARLING EDITOR RACHEL CARTER, FROM WHOM I NEVER HAD A CROSS WORD OR AN IMPATIENT MOMENT; NOTHING WAS TOO MUCH TROUBLE. YOUR WINGS AND HALO WERE A GIFT TO ME! THANKS ALSO TO NICOLA YOUNG FOR HER FANTASTIC WORK ON THE CONTRIBUTOR BIOS.

THANK YOU TO LUCY LEWIS, WHO PAINSTAKINGLY TESTED MANY OF THESE SCRUMPTIOUS RECIPES TO MAKE SURE THEY WOULD TRANSLATE DELICIOUSLY FROM AN ITALIAN KITCHEN INTO AN ANGLO ONE!

I'D ALSO LIKE TO THANK MY PUBLISHER JULIE (JEWELS) GIBBS FOR JOINING ME AT OUR PHOTO SHOOT ON THE AMALFI COAST. IT WAS SUCH AN HONOUR TO HAVE HER TALENT ON BOARD – SHE IS AN AMAZING MULTI-TASKER!

SIMON GRIFFITHS, YOU ARE THE BEST AND FASTEST SHOOTER. THANK YOU FOR ALL THE WONDERFUL PHOTOS AND YOUR EASY MANNER WITH ALL THE LOCAL TALENT – YOU MADE EVERY DAY JOYFUL!

FINALLY, A BIG THANKS TO THE ITALIAN FOOD IMPORTERS OF AUSTRALIA WHO KINDLY SUPPLIED ME WITH THEIR BEAUTIFUL PRODUCTS TO PHOTOGRAPH AND HELP OUR READERS FIND THE PERFECT INGREDIENTS TO EXECUTE THESE DELICIOUS RECIPES.

INDEX

LANTERN

Published by the Penguin Group
Penguin Group (Australia)
250 Camberwell Road, Camberwell, Victoria 3124, Australia
(a division of Pearson Australia Group Pty Ltd)
Penguin Group (USA) Inc.
375 Hudson Street, New York, New York 10014, USA
Penguin Group (Canada)
90 Eglinton Avenue East, Suite 700, Toronto, Canada ON M4P 2Y3
(a division of Pearson Penguin Canada Inc.)
Penguin Books Ltd
80 Strand, London WC2R 0RL, England
Penguin Ireland
25 St Stephen's Green, Dublin 2, Ireland
(a division of Penguin Books Ltd)
Penguin Books India Pvt Ltd
11 Community Centre, Panchsheel Park, New Delhi – 110 017, India
Penguin Group (NZ)
67 Apollo Drive, Rosedale, North Shore 0632, New Zealand
(a division of Pearson New Zealand Ltd)
Penguin Books (South Africa) (Pty) Ltd
24 Sturdee Avenue, Rosebank, Johannesburg 2196, South Africa

Penguin Books Ltd, Registered Offices: 80 Strand, London, WC2R 0RL, England

First published by Penguin Group (Australia), 2012

10 9 8 7 6 5 4 3 2 1

Design by Evi Oetomo © Penguin Group (Australia)
Photography by Simon Griffiths

Typeset in Gotham by Post Pre-Press Group, Brisbane, Australia
Colour reproduction by Splitting Image Colour Studio Pty Ltd, Clayton, Victoria
Printed and bound in China by 1010 Printing International Ltd

National Library of Australia
Cataloguing-in-Publication data:

Tabberer, Amanda.
Amalfi coast recipes / Amanda Tabberer.
ISBN: 9781921382482 (hbk.)
Includes index.
Cooking, Italian – Recipes.
641.5945

penguin.com.au/lantern